NOURISH:

GROW YOUR NUTRITION BUSINESS FROM THE GROUND UP

Written by: L. Nicole Marchand Aucoin, MS, RD

Founder & CEO of Healthy Steps Nutrition, CrossFit HSN & HSN Consulting

ISBN-13: 978-1978396333

ISBN-10: 1978396333

Dedication:

This book is dedicated to my mother, Inez Marchand, who was the most inspirational woman I have ever met. I'm forever grateful to her for being my life-long role model.

This book is also dedicated to my devoted husband, Jason Aucoin, who encouraged me to take a leap of faith in order to start this journey. His support led me to leave a secure, full-time position to grow my private practice. Thank you for being my sounding board for every idea and supporting my dreams.

NOURISH: 1

DEDICATION: 3

PROLOGUE 8

CHAPTER 1: WHY NUTRITION? 15

THE IMPACT OF NUTRITION 17
TAKING A LEAP INTO PRIVATE PRACTICE 19
BUILD YOUR EXPERTISE 21
CHOOSING YOUR PATH 24

CHAPTER 2: THE BIG PICTURE 27

CONSISTENCY WITHIN A SYSTEM 29
ROLES & TASKS 33
PRIOR TO PROGRAM LAUNCH 33
MARKETING 34
NUTRITION COACHING 35
NUTRITION CHALLENGES 36
BUILDING AWARENESS ABOUT YOUR BRAND 37
SAMPLE PACKAGES ON NUTRITION LANDING PAGE: 38
VALUE YOUR TIME 38
PRIVATE OFFICE VS. SHARED SPACE 40

CHAPTER 3: PHASE I - CREATING A CUSTOMIZED PLAN 44

DETERMINE YOUR CLIENT'S BASELINE 45
BRIGHT SPOT ENGINEER 48
BIOMETRICS 49
GOAL-SETTING 53
NUTRITION EDUCATION 54
THE FUNDAMENTALS 55
CREATING ACTIONS STEPS 63
FOOD LOGGING & PHOTO JOURNALING 65
AFTER THE CONSULTATION 66
RECOMMENDED PRICING STRUCTURE 68
OFFERING DISCOUNTS 69

WHAT HAPPENS NEXT 70
THE HSN SYSTEM 71
NUTRITION FOR RESULTS & RETENTION 72

CHAPTER 4: PHASE II - ACCOUNTABILITY AND ONGOING COACHING 73

ACCOUNTABILITY: A BUSINESS PERSPECTIVE 75
RECOMMENDED PRICING STRUCTURE 79
TOOLS FOR ACCOUNTABILITY 80
BIOMETRICS 80
JOURNALING 81
ACCOUNTABILITY PARTNERS 84
GOAL SETTING AND REWARDS 85
SETBACKS 88
PRODIGAL SONS 90
DRAWING THE LINE 92

CHAPTER 5: SHORT-TERM CHALLENGES TO LONG-TERM CLIENTS 96

TIMELINE FOR MARKETING A CHALLENGE 99
RUNNING A SUCCESSFUL NUTRITION CHALLENGE 102
INCREASING ENGAGEMENT DURING THE CHALLENGE 110
AFTER THE CHALLENGE 110
CHARGING FOR CHALLENGES 112

CHAPTER 6: THE RIGHT FIT TO RUN YOUR PROGRAM 114

CHOOSING A PARTNER 117
BRANDING YOUR NUTRITION PROGRAM 122
ADDING STAFF 125
COMPENSATION FOR NUTRITION COACHES 127

CHAPTER 7: MARKETING YOUR PROGRAM 130

MARKETING PLATFORMS 131
NO-SNACK INTRO 133
DECIDING WHAT TO POST 135
ANSWERS TO COMMON QUESTIONS OR PROBLEMS 135
RECIPES 136
SUCCESS STORIES 137
SOCIAL MEDIA TOOLS 142
HOW MUCH—AND WHEN—TO POST 144

Reviews 146
Delegate 148

CHAPTER 8: CREATING CONTENT 149

Email Marketing 150
Sample Love Letter 151
Newsletters 153
Sample Email Monthly Schedule: 155
Writing for Magazines & Journals 156

CHAPTER 9: ESTABLISHING PARTNERSHIPS 158

Partnership #1: Physicians and Pediatricians 160
Partnership #2: Meal Prep and Delivery Services 162
Partnership #3: Corporations 164
Partnership #4: Restaurants 166
Partnership #5: Teen Sports Teams 168
Other Partnerships 171
Finding Partners 173

CHAPTER 10: COMMON MISTAKES 178

Mistake #1: Lack of Resources 179
Mistake #2: Failure to Set Expectations, Part I 180
Mistake #3: Failure to Set Expectations, Part II 181
Mistake #4: Underestimating the Value of Content & Social Media 183
Mistake #5: Forgetting About Former Clients 184
Mistake #6: Not Valuing My Time 185
Mistake #7: Not Hiring a Mentor Sooner 187

Prologue

I was 13 when my mom was diagnosed with breast cancer. It was Valentine's Day. My parents called me and my younger sister to their bedroom and broke the news to us. We were too young to know what the "C" word meant, but we knew life was about change.

My mom was the most inspirational person I have ever known. In fact, in 2002, she was voted the most inspirational person in our hometown. She was known and loved by everyone in town. She started a flourishing private practice as a general dentist and was the president of the Junior League of Daytona Beach. She was busy running a business and helping anyone who crossed her path, all the while spending every second she could raising me and my sister. I can't remember a time that she didn't have a smile on her face. Even through the countless treatments, she focused on the positive. Her outlook on life was contagious.

After she was diagnosed, my mom opted for the usual treatments, including chemotherapy, radiation, and surgery. In 1999, we received the wonderful news that she was in remission. Unfortunately, the cancer returned less than two years later. The cancer had resurrected itself in her bones, and the prognosis was not good.

Doctors gave her only a few months to live.

This time around, she wanted to do things differently. My dad began researching alternative medicine and additional treatment options to supplement conventional medicine. Instead of fighting poison with poison this time, she chose to fight it with food.

My dad had read a copy of *Alive and Well: One Doctor's Experience with Nutrition in the Treatment of Cancer Patients* by Dr. Philip E. Binzel., Jr.; it became a roadmap for my mother's treatment. Dr. Binzel's recommendations included using food as medicine, and the root of his philosophy was focused on one simple concept: *clean eating.*

This became our family philosophy.

Although we'd always eaten relatively well (a dentist by trade, my mom enforced strict limits on sugar consumption), we filled our plates with organic vegetables, lean protein, and healthy fats. We cooked most meals at home, and there was no junk food in the house. If my sister or I wanted a snack, we snacked on vegetables and fruit.

The cancer did eventually claim my mother—she passed away in February of 2002—four years after the original diagnosis. Those were years beyond what the doctor had originally estimated; years I was able to spend with my mother.

But, my journey with food wasn't over. My mother's cancer affected my life forever. Observing how balanced nutrition positively impacted my mom's journey ignited my passion for health, wellness, and disease prevention.

Given my family's dietary overhaul while my mother was ill, it never occurred to me that my diet was anything short of exemplary. I ate leafy greens, not French fries, and I stayed physically active as a member of the high school cheer squad and then cheering in college at the University of Florida.

But like many young women, especially on the squad, in front of the crowds and cameras, I felt pressure to be thin. I began restricting my calories in hopes of getting as light and thin as possible, eating as little as one granola bar over the course of a day filled with cheer practices and games.

I had no energy and my performance tanked. Because of our eating habits, the coaches were rightfully concerned that some of the squad may be struggling with disordered eating habits. They took positive action and sent us each to meet with a dietitian.

The dietician showed me the link between my calorie deficit and my exhaustion. She taught me that in order for my metabolism to function, I needed to feed it. With my understanding came a new passion: I wanted to do for others what she was doing for me.

I changed my major the next day, and in 2010, graduated with a Bachelor of Science in Nutrition and Dietetics with minors in Leadership and Business. Since then, I've gone on to earn a Master of Science in the Science of Nutrition and completed a dietetic internship to become a Registered Dietitian (RD). I have also been privileged to serve a diverse population of people as an RD at multiple hospitals and as a private practitioner.

I love helping people make positive lifestyle choices, rather than just giving them a diet to manage disease. After that, I started volunteering at Lifestyle Wellness, a private practice in Gainesville, Florida. I spent the next four years working under the owner, trainer and RD, learning the ins and outs of the business. I was hired there as soon as I obtained my RD credentials.

In 2010, I discovered CrossFit. Founded by Greg Glassman in 2005, CrossFit is a fitness program defined on **www.crossfit.com** as "constantly varied functional movements performed at high intensity."

As a result of combining the CrossFit training methodology with a balanced diet focused on whole foods, today I eat 10 times more than I ever have in my life. At the same time, my body fat percentage is lower now than ever before.

But CrossFit didn't just influence my fitness; it changed my career as well. In 2012, I accepted a job as the only Registered Dietitian at a hospital in Boca Raton, FL. I wanted to get as much experience as I could with all different populations of patients. I joined a CrossFit in Deerfield Beach not long after. As I continued to train at the facility, athletes and coaches began to seek me out for nutrition advice. I began offering nutrition seminars at local gyms, while also building a private practice of my own.

In 2012, I opened Healthy Steps Nutrition (HSN) as my own private practice. I would see clients when I wasn't working in the hospital, and over time, I began also working with local gyms to help them with nutrition. I ran nutrition challenges all over the state of Florida. My goal was always to stop working in the hospital as soon as I built a sustainable business and income with the private practice alone.

I remember my first mentoring call with Chris Cooper, owner of Two-Brain Business, when he asked, "What does your perfect day look like?" It seemed like I was so far from that perfect day. I was starting my days at 4-5 am and wrapping up with clients or training at 7-8 pm. I was driving two or more hours daily between clients and the hospital. I wanted everything under one roof—I wanted to help people prevent disease, not fight it.

My husband pushed me to leave the hospital in 2014 and make HSN my full-time career. There were so many things to take into consideration, such as benefits, paid time off, set hours. It was a leap of faith and I'm forever grateful to him for pushing me to do it. I started partnering with local pediatricians, systemized my service, and expanded into coaching CrossFit.

Through HSN, my team and I offer individualized adult and pediatric nutrition programs, as well as gym consulting programs. We give gym owners all the tools they need to build and maintain a successful nutrition program.

In December of 2016, I expanded HSN by opening my own CrossFit gym, CrossFit HSN. At CrossFit HSN, we provide a comprehensive package of fitness and nutrition programming. Clients start with an initial assessment, learn the foundations of nutrition and fitness, and then continue with personal training or jump into group classes. At HSN, we test different ideas and strategies, perfect them, and then pass the best practices on to the gyms running our program.

Opening CrossFit HSN has allowed me to help our community at a new level. Clients come here for exercise on a daily basis, but we also discuss nutrition. It's the foundation of our philosophy and is what sets our gym apart from the 10 other gyms located within a five-mile radius of our facility.

Today, Healthy Steps Nutrition provides nutrition services for hundreds of gyms around the world.

This book outlines how we did it successfully.

Chapter 1: Why Nutrition?

The first five years of my career as a Registered Dietitian (RD), I worked at a hospital. My days consisted of meeting with 20 or more patients about how to manage their diseases. Often times, they were prescribed medications with drastic side effects to manage their diseases, but it never actually fixed the underlying issue: their lifestyle. The majority of these patients' health issues were directly related to a preventable disease. If they changed their eating habits, their health would improve.

I founded Healthy Steps Nutrition (HSN) to help people prevent disease. I wanted to educate people on how to make health a way of life, one step at a time. The HSN structured nutrition program provides people with the support they need to be successful long-term.

The HSN journey started small, as any successful business would, with nutrition counseling for individuals, group seminars, and personal training. Then, we moved to providing structured nutrition programs to Registered Dietitians, nutritionists, and fitness facilities who were unsure of how to implement their own program from scratch. In 2016, we opened a fitness facility that allowed us to have frequent contact with nutrition and fitness clients who were looking to make a life change.

We set out to provide nutrition counseling and fitness to the community, and that's exactly what we have done. Every person who walks through our doors talks to us about their current eating habits first, and we guide them with recommendations that are realistic for their life situation.

People need simple, actionable steps to help them achieve their goals and that is our philosophy for success. Every client starts by answering a series of questions to determine their baseline. Then we set realistic goals and create action steps so they feel confident implementing a plan when they aren't sitting in your office. Yes, you can tell them all about metabolism after six years of college, but your clients don't care about that. They need a plan to help them get from where they are at right now to where they want to be. It's your job to create that plan.

The Impact of Nutrition

As members of the health industry, our primary goal with anyone who comes to us looking to make a change is to help them develop a lifestyle that is healthy and fit. Professionally, we are not in the business of quick-fixes or fad diets. To make long-term changes, our potential clients need to understand how poor nutrition can impact their day-to-day lives. We need to show them that by eating correctly and exercising, we can decrease the likelihood of developing preventable diseases by large percentages.

As of 2014, 36 percent of adults and almost 20 percent of children between the ages of two and nineteen in the United States were overweight, according to the Centers for Disease Control and Prevention (CDC).[1] Worldwide, 2.8 million people die each year as a result of obesity or obesity-related diseases.[2] In addition to those statistics, studies show that people who do lose weight are unable to keep it off. One 2003 study found that 97 percent of its 2,400 participants regained the weight within two years.[3, 4, 5]

These findings are astounding, but what the results tell us is even more impactful. In 2017, the CDC reported that in 2014, approximately 40 percent of all cancers diagnosed were associated with being overweight or obese. Cancers related to excess weight include: esophageal, colorectal, endometrial, gallbladder, stomach, kidney, liver, ovarian, pancreatic, thyroid and postmenopausal breast cancers, as well as meningioma and multiple myeloma.[6] Therefore, as people struggle to lose weight and keep it off, their chances of developing these cancers increases.

There is also the societal mindset behind weight and weight loss. Because of the prevalence of obesity and obesity-related diseases, the market is saturated with pills, programs, and even surgical options promising to help us shed the weight. All of these options promise to fix the problem quickly, with little regard for side effects. These paths to weight loss can be dangerous for many, especially when people may not understand what they are putting in their bodies.

Now, imagine being able to impact just the smallest percent of that with your business. By helping a client develop a lifestyle of good nutrition, you will add years to their life and support their life goals through health. This is an incredible impact you can have on the life of many.

The research by the CDC proves that what we are doing is not enough. If prevalence of diseases can be reduced by reducing obesity, then we need to make a change in how people eat. This is where running an effective and consistent nutrition program plays a role.

Taking a Leap into Private Practice

I came to the realization that good nutrition is the foundation of all positive health changes. While your experiences may be different, there is still a reason you are in the field of nutrition, fitness, or both. At some point in your life, you chose to be healthy and help others do the same.

Starting a private practice is a big step for a dietitian. You may be in a comfortable situation with a set salary and leaving that brings a lot of unanswered questions. When starting a private practice, one of your potential fears is finding a client base to start with. You can start slow, and as you build a client base, you can leave the full-time position. That's exactly the path I took.

In other cases, you may be transitioning from a clinical setting to venture out on your own. While you may have studied how to treat disease, have you applied that information to clients looking to lose weight? Being aware of the mindset of potential clients is important, as it changes how you approach your business. You are the expert in dietetics, but your clients don't care about that. They care about how you can help them achieve their health and fitness goals and maintain a lifestyle change.

If you are a gym owner wanting to amplify your clients' results, balanced nutrition should be at the top of their priority list. I see many gym owners ignoring nutrition. The common reason nutrition is not prioritized at a facility is because gym owners and trainers feel uncomfortable discussing nutrition with their clients. Typically, this is an issue of expertise. Unless they have an academic or clinical background in dietetics, trainers often feel ill-equipped to offer nutrition recommendations.

In a gym setting, educating clients on nutrition is also time-consuming, and time is a scarce resource in the life of any business owner. The creation, implementation, and ongoing promotion of a nutrition program is a full-time job. Therefore, finding the right system for your gym, along with the correct person to run it, will reduce the number of hats you wear while improving your clients' results.

Regardless of whether you are a RD or gym owner, consider the reason many of your clients reached out to you for help. They were looking to make a drastic change in their life. In most cases, this is not the first step they are making to lose weight. They have tried different things in the past and now have decided to ask you for help.

In both situations, you are battling with conflicting mindsets. You are either changing the perception of potential clients so they value good nutrition and not fast results, or trying to teach coaches at your facility why nutrition must be a priority.

Build Your Expertise

If potential clients are going to place their nutrition in your hands, they must be confident that what you're telling them to do will yield results. You have to give your program authority. There are two ways to do this: You can be the expert or you can hire one. If you want to become an expert yourself, you have to do your homework. If you are already a RD, you need to feel confident helping the diverse population that will come to your practice.

There are multiple avenues available if you want to expand your nutrition experience. The Academy of Nutrition and Dietetics offers resources on a variety of nutrition-related subjects. You might also consider taking courses at a local community college. There are also private companies who offer online certification courses. You need to do your research to choose a reputable program.

If you have developed your expertise by obtaining your degree in dietetics, that is a great first step. However, you may not feel comfortable working with the populations that will seek you out in a private practice setting. In school, I learned very little about teen sports nutrition, and there wasn't much time spent on pediatric gastrointestinal issues. Yet, I found that those are two populations that I work with the most in practice. I developed my skills in those areas through continuing education units (CEU) to ensure I was an expert for my clients.

Nutrition, just like the fitness field, is constantly evolving, so it's important to stay up-to-date on the latest information for the health of your clients. While CEUs are required every year, it's important to focus on topics that will help you grow your private practice. You can also take one of the additional certifications offered through the Commission on Registered Dietitians on pediatrics, weight management, or sports nutrition. It will expand both your nutrition knowledge and provide you with strategies to help your clients.

However, these courses will not grow your business.

I remember searching for resources that would help with the opening of my private practice. There weren't many resources out there. This is what prompted me to write this book and start offering CEUs. I want to help you avoid making the same mistakes I did.

If you are not a RD, remember that these courses do not make you a dietician. The term "nutritionist" is not a recognized title. Laws regarding nutrition counseling vary by state, and scope of practice is something to keep in mind if you are not a dietitian looking to implement nutrition services. Specifically, there are two actions that can get you into trouble. In many states, it's illegal for anyone but a RD to write individualized meal plans for clients. In all states, medical nutrition therapy can only be done by a RD.

As tempting as it may be to try to hold all of the reins yourself, consider hiring a professional to guide the nutrition program at your facility. It took thousands of hours to create the system for nutrition and develop the resources and materials we give to our clients. As a new RD or fitness professional, do you have that amount of time to invest before launching your nutrition program?

Choosing Your Path

Regardless of whether you choose to run the ship or hire a professional, you need to determine your nutrition philosophy. There are many different fast action diets (FADs) out there: low fat, high fat, ketogenic, raw, whole foods, juices, flexible dieting, calorie counting, shakes, pills—the list goes on. All claim to be the most effective method for achieving ideal body composition.

Your clients don't need meal replacements, they need real food. They don't need a severely restrictive diet, they need a healthy lifestyle.

When determining a philosophy, the questions you need to ask yourself are:

- What's best for your clients?
- How much will they have to change?
- Will it realistically fit into their lifestyle?

Here is an example of how an untrained person providing nutrition advice can negatively impact someone's health. I once had a mother frantically call me because her teen daughter was placed on a diet from a local chiropractor, and she started having adverse effects. She pleaded that I see her daughter, Lisa, within the next day or two. Lisa was 17. When Lisa and her mom came into my office, I was shocked by what they said. Lisa had been placed on an 800-calorie diet after seeing a local chiropractor. The chiropractor told her to replace her meals with soy-based chips and bars that were sold at his office. She was not allowed to eat fruit and was permitted only one meal with protein and vegetables.

Lisa also ran a surf camp during the summer. She swam and surfed with children all day long for two months while following this restrictive diet. While Lisa lost weight, she started to have mood swings, low energy levels, and stopped getting her period. My client and her mother thought they were taking the right steps because they heard it from a doctor. We worked together over the next few weeks before she went back to school and put her on a sustainable plan to achieve her goals without severely restricting her diet.

During my studies, I took many courses about anatomy and physiology. I learned even more about the back and spine when taking training certifications. Does that mean I'm ready to perform adjustments? Definitely not.

Lisa is not the first client who has come to us after being placed on a very restrictive diet. One of the most popular blogs we wrote on our website, www.healthystepsnutrition.com, discussed how to identify if you are falling into a FAD diet trap, similar to the one Lisa was recommended.

Sadly, this happens more often than I would like to admit. Clients come to us after seeing an "expert" who encourages patients to purchase their products. This can be a dangerous path regardless of who they are hearing it from.

At the end of the day, it's your nutrition program, so you have to do the research as to what type of nutrition program you are going to recommend to your clients. The program created by Healthy Steps Nutrition that runs at hundreds of gyms worldwide focuses on balance. We discuss behavior modification and healthy habits over restricting food.

Chapter 2: The Big Picture

During 2013, I implemented nutrition challenges at gyms around the state of Florida. Gym members would see results, but after the challenge, they didn't have the support system in place to help them continue. Many challenge participants would reach out asking me to work with them remotely. When I arrived at CrossFit Port Orange and met with the owner, Sam, she expressed an interest in running a nutrition program—but she wanted more than just the challenge we were running at other gyms. She wanted to run our entire program remotely at her facility.

We had one major issue: there was no way she would know how to implement the program because I didn't have a system in place. I knew what to say to clients, how to answer their questions, how to create a customized plan, and what resources to provide. It was all in my mind. However, I didn't have a written blueprint on how to run the program because I was the only one running it.

I spent the next year creating a system to scale HSN and provide Sam with a structured nutrition program to run at her facility. Sam went from running no nutrition program to having a full schedule of clients with individual nutrition packages. People even drive over 20 miles to get nutrition coaching at CrossFit Port Orange.

Two years later, there are hundreds of gyms running the HSN program because of how easy it is to implement. The system has evolved over the years producing the gold standard for growing nutrition start-ups. We have helped RDs and fitness facilities see a 400%+ ROI by providing them a nutrition system that is ready to implement right away.

In this chapter, I introduce the overarching elements to run a successful nutrition business. Throughout the book, I will address each of these elements in depth, providing actionable steps to create a successful business model.

Consistency Within a System

When I talk to a RD or fitness owner about running our program, the roles and tasks description is the first thing I review. When creating a system, it needs to be easy for everyone to follow the same steps when meeting with clients. Roles and tasks ensure the backend of your system is running smoothly.

By having a playbook of exactly what to do, you are creating a structured system at your facility. This will allow you to expand, add staff, and grow your program exponentially because you aren't relying on one person to run everything. One of the most valuable resources we added to the "Get Free Help" tab on our website was the roles and tasks for a nutrition coach. If you are a RD starting or running a nutrition program, implementing roles and tasks will be helpful in ensuring consistency within your program. Think of these as the behind-the-scenes blueprint.

You need consistency behind the scenes and with your client experience for easy transferability. What happens if you stopped seeing nutrition clients today? Would someone be able to step in your shoes? Would they know what to do? This is why having a blueprint and a process for all aspects of your business is important.

The HSN system is set up in the form of an online course to ensure everyone is on the same page with the philosophy explained to clients. Everyone running our program, including the RD that I hired to help see our clients, completed the course. After that, nutrition coaches are provided a playbook--a breakdown of exactly what happens in each consult, what questions to ask, and how to respond to the most popular questions. There are estimated time increments so that coaches can keep the flow of the consults. These user guides make it easy for coaches around the world to run the nutrition program with the same structure.

When going to school to become a RD, you learn everything you could ever want to know about medical nutrition therapy and metabolism. Creating a system and resources wasn't part of the curriculum. It takes thousands of hours to create resources for clients. As you grow and evolve, your resources will too. We are constantly updating our materials to improve the client experience and help our clients in the best way possible.

Here are some questions to consider when starting a private practice and creating your system:

- How will you structure your nutrition programs?
- What questions will you ask your clients to ensure you get the full picture when talking to them for the first time?
- What resources will your clients walk away with?
- How will you track their progress?

- What sets your program apart?
- How often will you meet with clients?
- How will people find out about your service?

Over the past five years, I've worked with dietitians and hundreds of gyms who've come to me for guidance on how to develop a nutrition program. Over 90 percent have the same foundational problem: They lack a system.

Whether you are a dietitian looking to start a private practice or a gym owner, it is important to put nutrition science into a usable, digestible format, or your clients won't adhere to it. If your "nutrition program" is simply chatting about protein shakes or what your client is eating whenever you happen to see them, you are not providing the structure they need to reach or maintain their desired goals. You need a plan that includes a concrete system with replicable, actionable steps to keep both your clients and your nutrition coach on a track to measurable success.

There are many reasons why having a structured system is essential to the success of your nutrition program. They include:

- The program can be easily passed from one leader to another. You might begin by leading it yourself, but eventually you'll have too much on your plate and you'll need to delegate.
- Everyone at your facility needs to communicate the same plan. If you have one person preaching strict Paleo and

another person advocating for intermittent fasting, they're offering conflicting information, and your clients will be confused.

- Even if multiple nutrition coaches are on the same page, the program and all its components need to be consistent from client to client. If you come to me for nutrition counseling and your best friend comes two weeks later, the same thing needs to happen in both of those meetings. If your product is inconsistent, your results will be, too.
- Maybe you are a RD and have reached your capacity with clients. In order to ensure the same quality of service when you bring on another team member to help you with your client load, you need a system.

Creating a system will take additional time up-front, but if you partner with someone who has already created a structured system, such as HSN, it will take the burden off of you and allow you to focus on other aspects of growing the business. The structure not only shows professionalism on your end, but gives you a way to show numerical results to clients, which leads to retention.

You will also decrease the number of people who fall through the cracks. You will increase the awareness of your brand through consistent content produced. Creating a system allows you to establish a long-term growth plan for a sustainable business.

Roles & Tasks

The main task in running a nutrition program or practice is to breathe life into the program, to feed it, and cultivate clients. Therefore, that person needs to have a direct role in generating resources, marketing, and administration, in addition to actually meeting with clients. As a RD opening a private practice, this will be you in the beginning until you add on someone to help you see clients.

Here is the gold standard to follow when initiating your program launch:

Prior to Program Launch

- Ensure the website is running with your packages outlined
- Gather success stories to post on the website
- Create a "call to action" page on the website with a portal to purchase packages and book consults
- Send email content discussing WHY nutrition is important
- Create infographics with a call to action

What's Right For You?

Get your own customized plan, created for YOUR lifestyle & YOUR goals.
Our nutrition program is written and overseen by a Registered Dietitian!
Set up an appointment today!

Sample Infographic:

Marketing

- Post weekly nutrition tips on the website and social media
- Post weekly nutrition success stories on the website and social media, linking back to nutrition program landing page
- Post nutrition "Question of the Day" with tips in coaches' notes file for the daily workout
- Post weekly recipes on the website and social media
- Develop nutrition content for a monthly newsletter

Nutrition Coaching

- Set regular consultation hours and add them to scheduling software
- Confirm appointments 24-36 hours prior via email and/or phone call
- Create resource folders for clients
- Maintain physical and electronic files for each client, detailing struggles, bright spots, goals, action plans and client metrics
- Set follow-up appointments and send corresponding follow-up and reminder emails
- Review food logs
- Develop success story "highlight boards"
- Have success stories visible in your office or fitness facility of your nutrition clients.

Same Welcome Area Display:

Nutrition Challenges

- Create physical and electronic marketing materials
- Manage registration and biometric testing
- Plan and execute email marketing blasts
- Create and manage private a social media group for challenge participants
- Create physical folder of resources for participants
- Lead challenge kickoff seminar
- Post recipes and other content online
- Engage with clients in person and online
- Collect weekly tracker sheets
- Develop success story “highlight boards” for all participants
- Select and announce challenge winner

Of course, this is just a starting point. Over time, you will expand these roles and tasks to further develop your program. We will dive into each nutrition package and how to run a challenge later in this book.

In the coming chapters, we will discuss the elements of an effective program, how to expand on these roles and tasks, as well as how to maximize your return on the time you spend.

Building Awareness About Your Brand

We live in a society where the internet is the first place people turn to for help. Therefore, when launching a nutrition business, establishing a website is a priority. I designed my first website through a do-it-yourself program in 2011. It was only a temporary solution. Since then, I upgraded and hired a professional to create it. Your website is the first impression for potential clients.

Here is the information you need on your nutrition website:

- Your vision and mission
- The packages you offer
- Your pricing
- A way to sign up (we use a booking and billing software to manage all of our payments and scheduling)
- Success stories
- A blog for nutrition content
- "About You" page - your potential clients want to know WHO they will be working with
- A place to capture emails and build a list of people interested in your services

Sample Packages on Nutrition Landing Page:

JUMP START 1 MONTH	SHAPE UP 1 MONTH
$225	$350
• 80-Minute Initial Consultation • Customized Plan • Goal Setting • Client Handbook • Biometric Testing • One 30-Minute Follow-Up (In person) • On-going Support (Email) • Graduate to On-Going Coaching $75/month •	• 80-Minute Initial Consultation • Customized Plan • Goal Setting • Client Handbook • Biometric Testing • Two 30-Minute Follow-Up Visits (In person) • Weekly Accountability Check-In (Phone) • Weekly Food Log Review (Email) • Graduate to On-Going Coaching $75/month
BOOK TODAY!	BOOK TODAY!

Value Your Time

When starting out in the nutrition business, it is not uncommon for nutrition coaches to undervalue their time. If you are starting your own nutrition business, you may be tempted to offer lower prices to initially draw clients in. In a gym setting, you will have members coming to you at odd times to ask you nutrition questions. In both scenarios, you are eager to build awareness about your brand and may give away nutrition support for free.

Making a clear distinction between the services that you will and won't charge for is essential to maximizing your return on investment. You need to clearly state what is involved with each nutrition package being offered.

Imagine that you have set up your nutrition business and you have several clients texting you nightly, asking what they should eat the next day. Each conversation takes about 30 minutes. If you do this for four clients, that is equal to two hours each night where you are giving away nutrition coaching for free. Avoid this situation by clearly outlining up front the extent of your nutrition support.

When deciding what to charge, consider how personalized the service you are offering will be. Sending out content to your network and meeting with someone individually to help them on a more customized level come at very different costs to you. For example, social media posts and email blasts with nutrition tips should be provided to all clients or members for free because they come at minimal cost. Also, it develops your credibility in the field. Anytime you move from large-scale group efforts to one-on-one customized meal discussions, you want to charge or create boundaries.

Free Versus Paid Services:

Added Value for Clients (Free Services)	Chargeable Support and Resources
• Videos with tips • Recipes • Blog posts • Email content	• Food log review • Custom meal plans • Biometric testing • Creating plan

Private Office vs. Shared Space

After establishing your system, website, and preparing to launch, you will need to identify a place to see clients. A private space for nutrition clients is important because you want them to feel safe and secure when sharing their struggles. Nutrition and weight loss are emotional battles for most people. People use food to cope with stress in their life. There have been countless situations in the past where I have been talking to a client and they started to get emotional.

If I didn't have a safe, private space for clients to open up, I might not be able to help at a deeper level. If you have a private space to see nutrition clients, this will allow your clients to feel more comfortable and be honest.

If you do not have a private space to see clients, consider sharing space with another office during their off hours. If you are at a gym, you can schedule nutrition clients during the gym's off hours. Imagine trying to meet with a new nutrition client in the middle of a class with the music blaring. Show that you value their privacy by treating it as such.

For the first two years in private practice, I didn't have a home base where I would see all my clients. I would see clients out of the gym where I conducted personal training sessions. I would schedule appointments mid-day when the gym was slow or on the weekends when it was closed.

Weekends became a popular time to book appointments. If that didn't work, I went to clients' houses or met in another semi-private location. It wasn't the most ideal situation, but it worked.

There are many options when starting a private practice without the long-term commitment of a one- to five-year lease. There are shared work spaces. You can even rent a room for the hour or the day for as little as $20-30 per hour or $60 for the day. If I had to start all over again, I would set specific hours each month to host nutrition consultations and rent a shared space for a few hours or a day. This way, you aren't locked into a lease. As a starting dietitian, shared work spaces give you the flexibility to schedule when you want without the huge overhead.

Another option is sharing an office. In this case, be mindful of your clients' privacy. Set nutrition hours based on what your space will allow, and advertise those hours on social media, in newsletters, success stories, and emails. This will allow clients to book appointments easily.

Sample Nutrition Hours Advertisement:

Creating a system means planning out every step of the client experience. You need consistency from the moment a potential client decides to research nutrition on their home computer to implementation of the plan you created for them. These elements of the program must be determined before you see your first client.

At HSN, our system is divided into two phases: The initial assessment/plan development and ongoing coaching. Over the next two chapters, we will break down exactly what happens in Phase I and Phase II.

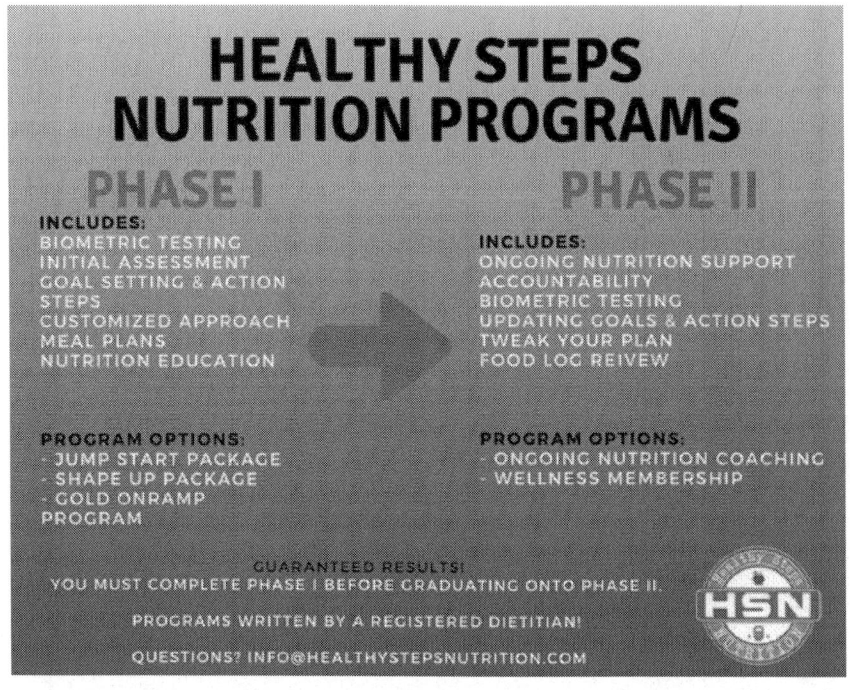

Chapter 3: Phase I - Creating A Customized Plan

Phase I of an effective nutrition program consists of an initial assessment and nutrition education. All nutrition clients go through a formal education process before jumping into an accountability and support program. Clients enter Phase I through individual customized plans or through a challenge. The goal of Phase I is to determine the client's baseline and start them on a plan to make long-term changes.

Determine Your Client's Baseline

Every nutrition client at HSN begins with an 80-minute, in-person consultation. This is where the client and nutrition coach get to know each other, take metrics, set goals, and develop their customized plan. They talk about the foundations of proper nutrition and behavior changes needed to achieve sustainable results. Keep in mind that your clients have done research prior to coming to you. Everything you could possibly want to know about nutrition is on the internet or in a book. Breaking down misconceptions and setting a foundation for lifestyle change is important during the first meeting.

The first portion of the initial consultation with a client should be question-focused. You do not want to throw a lot of information at them. The goal of the first portion is to get to know your client. Discovery questions include:

- What prompted you to make an appointment?
- What have you tried in the past?
- What are you hoping to accomplish?
- Do you have a medical history I need to be aware of?

While you are asking questions and your client is sharing their history, you should actively listen and take notes. The notes will help you develop a plan for your client, as well as create action steps aligned to their goals. We use an initial consult form to ensure we address all the important factors related to our client's success. The HSN initial consult form can be found in Appendix A.

In addition to asking why they're here and what they've done previously, we ask them these seven basic questions:

1. What do you eat on a typical day?
2. How often are you eating?
3. How often do you eat out, and where?
4. What kinds of liquids are you drinking?
5. Have you ever logged your food?
6. Are you taking any supplements?
7. How would you rate the quality of your current nutrition on a scale from 1-10?

As the client is speaking, determine if they feel like they are doing a good job. It is important to understand the client's perception of their own eating habits. Depending on where they are with their eating habits, you will create action steps. Their first step might be eliminating sugars and cutting portions, or it might be creating a detailed plan with specific macronutrients. Your clients need to feel confident when leaving your office, not overwhelmed. I love hearing, "This was easy!" from clients. That means we made great action steps to promote change.

You will also determine if a client has struggled with restrictive eating in the past. You do not want to put your client on a plan that could potentially lead to emotional or health issues. Therefore, to know where to start, you have to know where your client is mentally, as well as physically.

During this initial conversation, you need to find one bright spot—something the client is already doing right. Maybe a client is drinking several sugary supplement drinks throughout the day, but also eats a ton of vegetables. Take time to celebrate the fact that they are eating the vegetables. If the client is only hearing negatives about their current eating habits, they will not come back. When you find something they're doing right, they will be encouraged and more willing to makes changes. Success leads to motivation.

As you are reflecting with the client about their progress in the follow-up meeting, start with the bright spots, if possible. The first thing I say to client's during follow-up visits is, "Tell me all the awesome things you have done over the past couple weeks." The client will feel safer sharing their struggles if the meeting is positive at the very beginning.

This is also the time to get to know your client and establish trust. Before you start preaching about the evils of sugar, listen to their struggles and share a few of your own. Let them know that you know what it's like to experience challenges with nutrition and that it's possible to overcome them.

Bright Spot Engineer

Finding the actions your clients are doing right will increase their motivation. Bright spots are anything your clients are doing well in regard to nutrition habits. During Phase I and the initial consult, we draw attention to the bright spots in the determining your baseline conversation. Anything that a client is doing well, we acknowledge it. By bringing light to all the great things they are doing, they will be motivated to continue.

We begin every follow-up visit with clients listing all the positive changes they have made since our last visit. Sometimes, clients might not remember all the small changes they made. That's when we review the actions steps to see what they implemented.

When the plan is implemented properly, action steps turn into bright spots, then new goals and action steps are created the next month. Every month, action steps will be tweaked depending on what is going on with the client and the time of year. If it is during the holidays, you might devise action steps related to surviving the holidays and staying on track during the toughest time of the year.

Biometrics

After you develop a relationship with the client, you can approach taking metrics. This is vital for setting realistic goals and tracking progress. Consider what people are accustomed to hearing on television and reading on magazine covers: "Lose 10 pounds in 10 days," or "How I Lost 30 Pounds in a Month!" Clients might have unrealistic expectations of drastic weight loss that are not sustainable in the long run.

Comprehensive metrics provide you with multiple opportunities to identify success points with your clients. For example, a client comes in and has lost three pounds during their first month implementing the nutrition plan but was expecting drastic results. When redoing measurements, you determine that the client lost 17 inches. It's easy to find a bright spot with comprehensive metrics.

Take your traditional new gym client, someone who perhaps has been sedentary for years before joining the gym. It's not uncommon for that client to lose fat and simultaneously build muscle, resulting in a stationary scale needle and discouragement for the client. In reality, their body composition has improved for the better, but if you don't have the metrics to show them that improvement, they're likely to quit.

At HSN, we measure body weight, but it's just one metric of many.

Here's a list of what we test at HSN:

- Weight
- Body fat
- Muscle mass
- Water retention
- Inches at 8 different spots on the body

For the first 10 years of my private practice, I used a handheld machine to measure body fat percentage. The handheld machine sends a low electric current through the body to determine body water content. Muscle, blood vessels, and bones easily conduct electricity while fat does not. Then, it compares that number to a bank of statistics for a person of the same height and weight. Because muscle cells store more water than fat cells, the machine uses those statistics to produce an estimation of muscle to body fat percentage. Someone with a higher water content than another person of the same height and weight is estimated to have more muscle.

Another tool for measuring body fat is body fat callipers. Using body fat callipers is not the gold standard of practice because of the negativity they carry with them. Body fat callipers actually pinch a client's fat to measure the amount. Imagine being embarrassed about how far you let your body go as you walk into a facility for the first time for a nutrition consultation. You aren't comfortable, and it was a big step for you to even set up an appointment and walk through the doors. You would not be comfortable having someone pinch your stomach and back fat.

A handheld bioelectrical impedance machine is a great starter machine, but it's limited data points and reliance on statistics produce incomplete results. At HSN, we use a machine that gives a comprehensive measure of fat, muscle, and water levels in less than a minute.

The machine we use works similarly to the handheld bioelectrical impedance, however, it uses eight data points and multiple frequencies relying only on direct measurements instead of a built-in set of statistics. It measures body fat and lean muscle mass, which it breaks down by body segment as well as total percentage. By using a comprehensive machine, we track clients' progress in much greater detail to ensure they are on the right track.

A comprehensive machine is an investment, but it will pay for itself in the long run because it shows true results of various measures. For example, I had a client who had been training with CrossFit consistently for about eight months. She was doing great with her gym consistency and had lost some weight, but she wasn't seeing results as fast as she wanted. I began working with her on her nutrition. She saw little weight change over the next ten weeks. However, her biometric testing results revealed she had lost four percent body fat during that time.

Just as body fat percentage shows progress where the scale doesn't, inches typically drop faster than body fat percentage. At HSN, we take eight separate measurements using a flexible measuring tape: around the torso, one inch below the right and left shoulder, at the chest, waist, hips, and around each arm (at the midpoint between the shoulder and elbow) and each leg (six inches above the knee). There is a sample biometric tracking sheet in Appendix B. When progress seems to have stalled, those inches lost are the bright spots clients need to stay motivated. *Remember, success leads to motivation.*

The client I mentioned above who wasn't making progress at the rate she hoped according to the scale had actually lost three inches in her waist. The inches she lost were the bright spot. She said to me during her next consult, "This is exactly what I needed. I can do this." Your clients need encouragement. It's your job to be that cheerleader helping them. The more data points you have, the more likely you are to find a bright spot.

The gold standard for biometric retesting is every two to four weeks for individual coaching. Group challenges might only have biometric testing at the beginning and end of a four- to six-week challenge. When measuring biometrics, it is important to remember to look at weight, body fat, measurements, and muscle mass, not just one of those numbers.

Measurement Type	How Often
Measurements	Bi-weekly to monthly
Body Fat	Bi-weekly to Monthly
Weight	Weekly to monthly

Goal-Setting

With metrics in hand, you have the information needed to set realistic goals. When setting goals with clients, let them determine what they want to achieve, but guide them with a realistic time frame. Follow the SMART guide when setting goals:

- S: Specific
- M: Measureable
- A: Attainable
- R: Realistic
- T: Time-Sensitive

We also encourage clients to keep their goals visible. They could write them on a note stuck to the fridge or keep them as the wallpaper on their phone. The goals must include measurable milestones like body fat percentage, but they shouldn't be limited to that. The focus is about achieving overall wellness and that means actions taken outside the gym and off of the scale as well.

I had another client who owned a large business. He wanted to lose weight, but his main goal was to achieve the mental clarity that comes with clean eating and regular exercise. He wanted to be at his sharpest every time he sat down to work. Whenever we met, we discussed his progress toward that goal, ranking his mental clarity on a scale of 1-100 percent and tweaking what he put in his body like Omega-3 intake, raw foods, water intake, as well as time between meals. He started at 60 percent and is now sustaining a 97-100 percent when asked about mental clarity.

How you fuel your body goes way beyond achieving biometric goals. It's important to ask your client about energy levels, recovery, sleep patterns, and stress management. All play a vital role in your client's success.

Nutrition Education

Once goals are created, you should begin talking about nutrition and educating the client on your philosophy of nutrition. This connects directly back to having a consistent and structured system. You need to have concrete information, including physical resources, for the client to walk away with. If you verbally throw a bunch of information at them and have no materials for them to refer back to, they won't be able to follow the plan. They will be so overwhelmed by all the information that they're going to say, "I can't do this," and give up.

To ensure a seamless process, prepare folders in advance to give to clients. The contents of the folders may vary slightly by client depending on the level of customization they have purchased, but all will have the same foundational elements.

Folder contents:

- Information about the three macronutrients—protein, carbohydrates and fat, and how they affect the body
- Lists of healthy foods in each macronutrient category
- Meal plans (with varied levels of customization depending on the package)
- List of the client's goals and action steps to reach those goals
- A three-compartment container for visual illustration of macronutrient ratios per meal

---

The Fundamentals

At HSN, we prescribe clients to follow the macronutrient structure of the Zone Diet, developed by Dr. Barry Sears. We recommend clients start with 40 percent of daily caloric intake requirements coming from low glycemic carbohydrates and 30 percent each from protein and fat. It is the 40/30/30 system. This is how we design our meal plans for all of our clients.

In Barry Sears' book *Enter the Zone,* Dr. Sears discusses how having the appropriate macronutrient ratios will optimize hormone levels. He talks about how eicosanoids control hormone production, which in turn control all your body's hormonal systems such as the cardiovascular, immune, reproductive, and central nervous systems. He goes on to discuss the role of low- versus high-glycemic carbohydrates and their effects on the body.

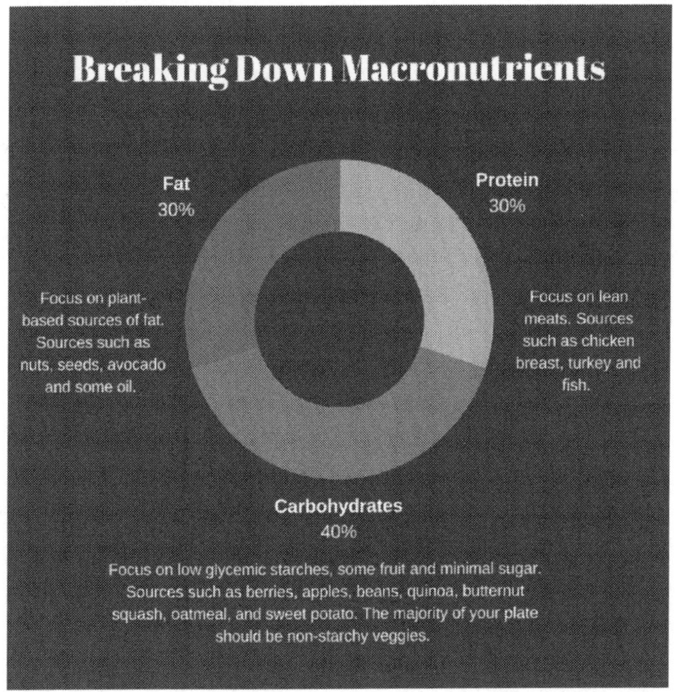

This philosophy is the basis of our meal plans, but we don't dive into the science with clients. Clients need to know how to get from point A to point B. Your job is to give them a map of how to get there.

One interesting situation that we see a lot is related to quantity not quality. A client is eating all the correct foods, but in the wrong portions. They aren't seeing the results they want and become frustrated with their efforts to achieve weight loss goals. On the opposite end of the spectrum, there are clients who eat terribly, but only a small amount. They might lose weight, but don't feel the best. That is why you need both: quality and quantity.

What you eat affects more than just your weight and how you look. Your body is a machine; giving it quality fuel will help it run better and longer, and the right quantity of those quality foods will help it run at its best.

When meeting with clients, I don't discuss the Zone Diet; rather, we use this system as the foundation of our meal plans. When talking with clients, we focus on sticking with whole foods and quality macronutrients. Our goal is that clients will not turn to the processed foods as staples in their diets. We want clients to focus on whole foods and shop the perimeter of the grocery store. Some programs or diet plans promote cutting out an entire food group. We always steer clear of this as every food group has an important role in the body.

Let's use fruit as an example. Fruits are great sources of vitamins and minerals. Cutting out fruit would decrease your body's ability to get those vitamins and minerals. Yes, fruit has sugar. Some fruits have more sugar than others, but some fruits also have more fiber than others. We recommend clients focus on the fruits with low sugar and high fiber content. Berries are low in sugar, high in fiber and loaded with vitamin C, fiber, folic acid, zinc and antioxidants. This is an example of how cutting out an essential food could make it difficult to meet requirements of micronutrients such as vitamin C.

Using the 40/30/30 system as a starting point, we customize plans while keeping the foundation the same from client to client. The specifics vary by individual. For example, an elite athlete may require more carbohydrates than a Type 2 diabetic, but the foundation of the program remains the same. It all comes down to the prevention of chronic disease.

The 40/30/30 system, when implemented with an eye toward quality of macronutrients and not just quantity, will yield results. In fact, we guarantee that our clients will reach their fitness and weight loss goals when implementing the program correctly. Quality means recognizing that 100 grams of broccoli and 100 grams of donuts do not have the same reaction in the body. Once clients understand both quantity and quality, we will decrease their risk for preventable diseases such as metabolic syndrome. Metabolic syndrome is a group of conditions that includes increased blood pressure and high blood sugar. Together, these conditions increase the risk of heart disease, stroke, and diabetes.

When discussing nutrition with clients, do not assume your clients are already familiar with what macronutrients are and how they work. Thanks to marketing, there's a lot of confusion in the public as to what healthy looks like. Sugary cereals are labeled heart-healthy because they contain whole grains. In fact, parents have brought their children to me and proudly revealed that they drink three juice boxes per day thinking it was a great substitute for fruit. One eight-ounce serving of apple-flavored Juicy Juice contains 26 grams of sugar. This is the same sugar content as an eight ounce can of Coca-Cola.

It's your job to educate clients without making them feel stupid. Instead of saying, "Oh no, juice boxes have just as much sugar as Coke! Why would you give three juice boxes to your child?" You might say, "This is a really common misconception. A lot of people don't realize this, but juice boxes can contain as much sugar as a

It's better to consume fruit in whole-food form so we ber and micronutrients with less sugar per serving."

Then, during your conversation, you can demonstrate how healthy eating isn't as foreign as they might think. Using the list of example foods from each macronutrient category, I have clients circle all the foods they like. Usually, they're surprised at the variety of foods we encourage them to eat; it's not just chicken and broccoli. The list can serve as a resource for creating healthy meal plans based on foods they already enjoy. The list also serves the additional purpose of showing clients what can serve as healthy substitutes.

The lists that HSN provides clients has proteins on the first page, carbohydrates on the second, and healthy fats on the third. For foods that contain two macronutrients, like Greek yogurt, the item would be on the list containing the primary micronutrient. Greek yogurt would be on the carbohydrate list. Nuts are listed on the fat list, although they do contain some protein.

When teaching clients how to interpret the meal plans, talk about pairing one food from each page to get the balance of protein, carbohydrates, and fat. This visual allows them to understand and create balanced meals on their own. After all, the goal is that they know what to do if they don't have chicken one day and the meal plan calls for chicken. You will also empower them to be creative while eating out to stay on track.

For clients with specific dietary choices, such as vegetarians, it is good to talk about macronutrient alternatives that fit into their lifestyle. Beans might be a source of protein, but to get the amount of protein you would need in a meal from beans, you would also double or even triple the amount of carbohydrates consumed. A vegetarian client might think that by adding nuts to a salad, they are getting a substantial amount of protein. In reality, they're adding more fat than protein. These are the small details that even someone who has done a lot of research could miss.

Finally, you want to discuss why the foods on those lists are good choices. I like to talk about how choosing lean sources of protein leave room for plant-based sources of fat, which will add more substance to the meal. I also address how loading up on non-starchy vegetables before the rest of the meal will help fill you up faster and keep you satisfied longer.

Inevitably, during these conversations, you'll have to do a little myth busting. For instance, explain to clients that trail mix loaded with dried fruit might not be the best snack option because it is often loaded with sugar and is not nutrient dense. "I thought trail mix was healthy," they exclaim.

This is a great opportunity to illustrate how not all calories are equal. In this instance, I explain to the client how nuts might have more calories than the cookie, but the way your body responds to the nuts is quite different. The cookie—high in sugar and refined carbohydrates—will cause a near immediate insulin spike and contribute to inflammation. The sugarless nuts will keep blood sugar levels stable, and the healthy fats they contain will keep you satisfied longer.

You will find in your experiences with clients that people don't know how they are designed to feel. Think about that. If all you know is junk food and convenience items, you don't know what it feels like to load up on fresh produce and quality foods. One time, one of our athletes came in to measure his body fat. We did a body composition scan on him and it showed his weight had gone down slightly. His muscle mass had increased, but also only slightly. He had been working very hard in the gym, and he thought his results would be better. So, we had a conversation about his eating.

During the conversation, I found out he was eating zero fruits or vegetables, so I encouraged him to start eating one to two cups with lunch and dinner. Two days later, he walked in the gym almost giddy with excitement. "I feel amazing!" he yelled.

Maybe it was the combination of all the sugary treats that he cut out or how he started incorporating vegetables. Either way, he had more energy, was feeling better, and was ready to push himself even harder to see the results he wanted.

Once the client has a basic understanding of the foundations of nutrition, they'll be better prepared to take on the action steps that will lead them to their goals. Action steps are paramount because without them, goals are still intangible dreams.

Creating Actions Steps

Consistency with your system but flexibility with your approach; that should be your motto. Creating goals and action steps is where the customization comes in for the client. Action steps will look different for every client, and even clients with similar goals will have different steps based on where they are in their journey to better health.

This is where it becomes important to have notes from the first part of the consult when you determined your client's baseline. You want to refer back to exactly what they are doing now to help create a roadmap of where they need to go. The principles remain the same—you want all your clients to eat healthily and consistently—but in practice, you need to be flexible with clients based on where they're starting from.

I once had an obese client who was accustomed to eating out at a buffet-style restaurant for lunch and dinner, every single day. Now, imagine if I told him that not only did he need to change what he was eating, but he also needed to begin preparing all of his meals at home. The change would be so drastic that he might have a couple of days of success before becoming overwhelmed. He may not have even started.

Instead, action steps for this client included:

1. Choosing three non-buffet restaurants with healthier menu options.
2. Making a list of which dishes were the best options to choose from. We also tried to send him to the restaurants we have partnered with locally, who already have dietitian-approved entrées on our menu.
3. Pack healthy snacks to keep from getting too hungry and overeating throughout the day.
4. Cut out lemonade and juice and switch to water.

Obviously, we don't want this to be the endpoint for any client, but you have to crawl before you can walk. These changes cut his calorie intake in half simply by virtue of eliminating the two-portion-per-meal buffet.

Another example of setting appropriate action steps concerns alcohol. Ideally, we do not want clients to drink alcohol. There is no nutritional benefit to alcohol. It's empty calories and often contains a lot of sugar and promotes inflammation. But, if a client is used to drinking in excess, going cold turkey is an action step they are unlikely to follow.

I once had a client who loved rum runners—a drink made of two kinds of rum, fruity liqueur, grenadine, and three different fruit juices. Depending on how it's made, it can have anywhere from 30 to 60 grams of sugar per serving. My client would drink 13 in a weekend. That's more than 100 teaspoons of sugar over two days.

The World Health Organization recommends limiting sugar intake to less than 25 grams, or six teaspoons, per day.[7]

I wasn't going to tell this client that he couldn't drink. For him, that's not realistic. Recommending to him to go from 13 drinks to zero would set him up for failure. A better action step was to switch from rum runners to a vodka soda or vodka water with lemon and lime and alternate the drinks with a glass of water. This way, he took a step toward reducing his alcohol intake without feeling deprived, and at the same time, he drastically reduced his sugar intake.

When creating action steps, you need to lay out for your clients the realistic steps to help them achieve their goals. Triage negative actions and focus on the actions your clients can take to make the most amount of change. Those are achievable action steps they can tackle first.

Food Logging & Photo Journaling

For most clients, food logging will be an action step at some point in their journey. It's an important component of accountability, which is discussed in a later chapter. Although it can be time consuming, food logging helps clients really understand what they're eating.

Food logs also play an important role in the quality of service a nutrition coach can provide. If a client comes back to me for a follow-up appointment after their first month and doesn't see the results they expected, I will not be able to provide feedback unless I can look at what they have been doing. In their food log, regardless of if its paper or electronic, clients should include:

- Food item
- Portion size
- Type of meal (breakfast, lunch, dinner or snack)

If logging specific foods and portion sizes is a challenging step for a new client, another option is to have the client take a photo of the meal. You will be able to see what they ate and what the portion size looked like. From there, you can provide feedback.

After the Consultation

Once a client has completed their initial consultation, we'll set a time and date for their follow-up appointment, typically two to four weeks later. However, that doesn't mean there will be no communication with the client for 30 days. Periodic check-ins will keep them on track and ensure they will see results when they return.

The moment the client leaves your office after their consultation, it's time to organize your notes and draft your follow-up emails. Here's where it will benefit you to have an automated system. When you first launch your program, you will be able to manage scheduling and follow-up calls and emails. Once your practice grows though, you'll need to automate those processes.

The Phase I packages are displayed clearly on our website. Clients know exactly how much follow-up they will receive and when to expect our points of contact. You can learn more about it by visiting my website at **www.healthystepsnutrition.com**.

During all in-person consultations, whether it's that first meeting or subsequent follow-up visits, I take handwritten notes. I do not stare at a computer screen to type while I have a client sitting in front of me. Those notes go in a file in my office, and once the client is gone, I enter the client's goals and action steps into an online file.

Then, I send an immediate follow-up email, thanking the client for coming in and summarizing what we talked about. The email reiterates the client's goals and action steps. It also reminds them to send me their food log and gives them the date of our next appointment. A similar email is scheduled to go out two weeks later. I will also take the time to draft an appointment reminder email and schedule it to be sent the day before the client's next appointment.

For my own organization, I keep my appointment calendar and client notes in the same system, an online scheduling program that allows me to keep client profiles, schedules, and billing

, all in one centralized place, accessible anywhere. If your on is accessible online, from any location, then it will be eas, respond quickly to a client. There are a number of similar programs out there; the key is to stay organized so you don't find yourself overbooked and overwhelmed.

Recommended Pricing Structure

Phase I – Sample Packages	
Components	Pricing
Four-Week Plan • Two in-person visits • Biometrics at the beginning and end • Customized meal plans • Goal-setting • Action steps • Physical resources	$199-$250
Six-Week Plan • 3 in-person visits • Weekly phone follow-ups and food log review • Biometrics at the beginning and end • Customized meal plans • Goal-setting • Action steps • Physical resources	$350-399

Offering Discounts

Three years ago, I did not value my time. I thought more clients meant more money for the business. I didn't have consistent prices and offered discounts to almost everyone, including couples. It took me too long to realize more clients didn't mean more money, it meant more time. Time is money.

The topic of couple's discounts for nutrition programs is brought up frequently with dietitians, gym owners, and on social media groups. I can understand the thought process; couples are eating the same food. It's only one plan, right?

We know an individualized approach ensures clients will be successful long-term. Each client should walk away with their own customized plan, goals, action steps, and meal plans. They might be eating the same foods, but the portions are different because their needs are different. When determining your prices, you need to look at the time investment beyond just the in-person visits. You might not be with a couple exactly double the amount of time during the in-person visit. However, you need to take into account the time you will be spending following up via email, reviewing food logs, and touching base with each individual.

Consider the logistics of couples' ongoing nutrition coaching--what happens if they can't come together to a consult? One of two things will happen: one of the clients will lose out on the most important part of the process—accountability, or you aren't being paid appropriately for your time if you are scheduling a second consult to accommodate the other person's schedule.

The gold standard for nutrition coaching is an individualized approach. Be clear with how your packages are laid out. Structure your program to help your clients see the best results and they will sing your praises forever.

What Happens Next

After a client's first four to six weeks, they are ready to move onto Phase II, or ongoing nutrition coaching. For two years, I ran HSN on monthly packages. Clients would sign up for one month, and they would be done after that month. During that first month, I would meet with a client, set goals, and test biometrics. After the first month, some people would come back for a follow-up and most would not. There was no system for continuation. It was not going to be a sustainable business model. Every month, I was starting at zero with clients.

Once I decided to change to the model, I focused on retention and ongoing nutrition coaching. I added Phase II, which is a maintenance plan that is discussed with clients from day one. Now, clients are not only focused on short-term results; they have a long-term plan. Clients come to you because you are the expert. It's your job to show them how you will help them with a long-term plan promoting a lifestyle change through accountability and ongoing support.

The HSN System

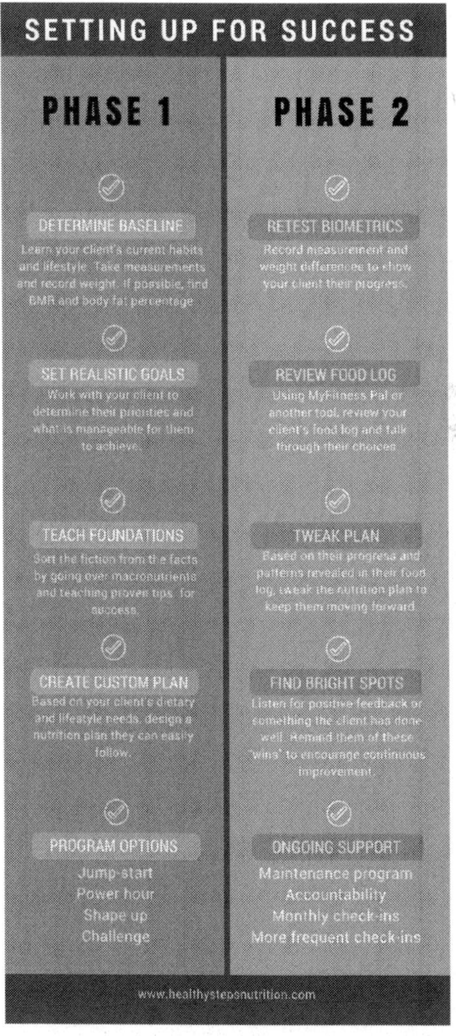

Nutrition for Results & Retention

As a business owner or potential business owner, you are constantly reflecting and adjusting the process to meet your clients' goals and improve client experience. This is why we transitioned to a Phase I and Phase II program. When we stopped talking about a six-week program and started discussing Phase I and Phase II, clients saw us as part of their long-term plan.

Clients who choose to transition to ongoing coaching see the value of accountability. We aren't trying to "sell" them more services; accountability and a support system is an integral part of their success. If your clients are seeing results at the rate that they hoped, they will stay on long-term. They will also refer their family and friends.

Chapter 4: Phase II - Accountability and Ongoing Coaching

As the nutrition expert, your product is more than your expertise. That's an integral part of what you offer, but it's not the only component of nutrition counseling. You must also provide accountability. An article released by the *Journal of Clinical Nutrition* states that only 12 percent of dieters in the study were able to maintain 75 percent weight loss after a three-year follow-up.[3] The study also showed that over 40 percent of people regained more weight than they initially lost.[3] Losing weight isn't the toughest part for your clients, it's keeping it off. However, if they have an accountability system in place when temptation strikes, they are more likely to stick with the plan.

I made the mistake of neglecting the importance of accountability when I first started working in private practice over 10 years ago. I would sit down with clients and provide the information they needed to be successful, but I didn't have a concrete plan for following up with those clients. More often than not, their results were lackluster, and I retained less than 10 percent of clients past the first month.

Now, using the system outlined in Chapter 3 and the tools for accountability outlined in this chapter, more than 75 percent of clients who start nutrition counseling at HSN stay beyond the three-month mark. Think of it like a fitness competition or any sort of high-stakes performance situation. When you sign-up for a competition, you're much more likely to train harder—or at least more consistently—because you know a day is coming when you'll have to perform. And, if you haven't trained for it, you're not going to perform well.

It's the same philosophy with nutrition. As my nutrition client, if you know that I am going to call you next week to discuss your progress and review your food log, you're more likely to stick with the plan. You are also more likely to log your food knowing that I'm going to review it every few days. The gold standard for setting up the next visit is while the client is in your office.

However, it is important to keep in mind that accountability is not about intimidation. If a client's success depends on not wanting to disappoint you or from fear of your reaction, they're not going to be successful for long. Accountability is about being supportive. People are more willing to stick with a plan if they know they have a cheerleader on their side.

Your job is more than asking if they followed through with what they said they were going to do. It is also about helping your clients see those bright spots—the small successes that will motivate them to continue—and facilitating the conversations they need to stay on track.

Accountability: A Business Perspective

The goal with any initial nutrition package is to convert the client to ongoing nutrition coaching. Since most people who lose weight don't keep it off, your clients need to be with you for the long haul, and it's important to be clear with them from the start that this isn't a short-term solution. It's a lifestyle change, and you're going to be with them every step of the way.

The system you establish, as we discussed in Chapter 3, ties directly into accountability. You need a good support system, and you need to be clear about how that support system works with your nutrition program. Setting expectations and explaining how you will help your client on their journey is going to be much easier for retaining clients beyond Phase I or the nutrition challenge.

As discussed in Chapter 3, the first action step you must take immediately following any client session is to send a follow-up email. In this email, you provide a recap of what was discussed in the session and what action steps the client will take moving forward. This is a great time to reiterate successes and bright spots, as well as indicate your enthusiasm and commitment to helping the client reach their goals.

Sample Email:

"Hey Susan,

I'm so excited to help you achieve your goals of losing weight and getting back into your skinny jeans! You've done a great job increasing your protein and water intake over the past two weeks.
For the next two weeks, let's focus on:

- *Adding more fresh vegetables with lunch*
- *Reaching the goal of drinking 80 ounces of water per day*
- *Remember to bring those awesome snack options we discussed*

Remember to send me your food log in two weeks, and I'll see you next month for our follow-up visit on July 3rd at 10AM!"

This is also the time to schedule check-in emails and remind your client to send food logs every two weeks. These may seem like small steps, but these emails are a big part of your accountability system. They give your clients reassurance that you're right there with them and focused on helping them reach their goals.

The reminder emails shouldn't be the only communication you have with your clients between sessions. You need to be specific from the beginning about how much contact is included in the package a client has chosen and expected turn-around time. The gold standard for email contact is to respond within 24 hours. Otherwise, you will have clients calling you every day when you're only charging for two sessions per month.

However, this doesn't mean you have to limit in-person contact to two sessions per month. The amount of accountability needed is different for every client, and you can work with your client to establish what works best for them. By offering different levels of packages, you are able to accommodate the clients looking for more accountability, and you will be paid appropriately for your time. You can see the nutrition packages we offer, as well as how they are structured and priced on our website: **www.healthystepsnutrition.com**.

In general, most of my clients are successful with a weekly email and a monthly in-person session. However, I had a distance client who requested a 30-minute phone call every single day to keep her on track. For this client, the extra accountability is worth the extra cost to ensure her success.

When putting together your on-going nutrition packages, start with a standard package offering one nutrition follow-up per month and bi-weekly email. Then, offer a deluxe ongoing coaching package offering two nutrition follow-ups and weekly emails. From there, you can make adjustments based on client needs, adding phone calls, scheduled consistently, or extra meetings as the client feels necessary. Your time is valuable and you should be compensated for it.

I recommend avoiding text communication as an option. When I first started offering nutrition counseling, I didn't mind all the text messages. Once my private practice started to grow, people were texting me at 10 p.m. and expecting a response immediately. Limiting communication to email and/or scheduled phone calls and establishing communication expectations from the start reinforces necessary boundaries to keep clients from taking advantage of you.

Recommended Pricing Structure

Phase II – Monthly Ongoing Nutrition Coaching	
Components	Pricing
Standard Package • Monthly biometrics • Bi-weekly emails or phone call check ins • Meal plan adjustment • Goal-setting • New action steps	$50-$79 per month
Deluxe Package • Bi-weekly biometrics • Weekly emails or phone call check ins • Meal plan adjustment • Goal-setting • New action steps	$100-150 per month

Tools for Accountability

Biometrics

So, practically speaking, what does accountability look like?

First, we have to consider the purpose of accountability. Accountability ensures a client sees progress. In order to ascertain whether progress is being made, you need measurable data. Therefore, the first tool in your accountability toolkit goes back to something we discussed in Chapter 3: biometrics.

During the first consultation with your client, you'll measure biometrics, including body fat percentage, body weight, and physical measurements. These aren't just numbers to have for a before-and-after comparison; they are guideposts to be used along your client's entire journey.

The gold standard is to measure body fat percentage once a month, but no more than twice per month. Physical measurements are done during in-person client follow-up sessions, once to twice per month. Inches drop faster than other biometrics, which leads to bright spots and successes for your client's progress. Although taking measurements can be tedious, it is one of the most valuable biometrics to keep your clients motivated to continue.

Additionally, clients shouldn't weigh themselves daily, but a weekly weigh-in is fine, provided it's done at a consistent time of day. The ideal time for weighing in is first thing in the morning to eliminate variables like food and water intake. These metrics are like road signs; they let you know if your client is on the right path and whether something in their plan needs to be tweaked. Biometrics hold your client accountable to their goals.

Journaling

Food logs function in much the same way. I see a direct correlation with clients who track their food and the rate of their progress. Clients think twice about what they're eating if they know they have to write it down.

Food logging applications make food logging easy. This is a great starting point for any client. We encourage the use of an application, instead of writing it down manually, because it will show the client the breakdown of calories and macronutrients of what they are eating in real time. If a client doesn't want to use technology, a notebook is a secondary alternative. The key is that they're not just writing down what they ate, but how much they ate as well. If that's too time consuming, have your client do a photo journal of what they are eating. A picture will provide you insight into their habits and portion size. It's not the best option, but it's better than not having a visual to review with them.

In most instances, if a client is not seeing results, it's directly correlated to what they're eating. If they haven't logged or photographed what they've eaten, how can you help them make adjustments? Human memory is fallible, and often selective. It's easy to forget about the handful of chips consumed at the office party or the sugar in your coffee. You can't rely on clients to accurately remember everything they consumed without keeping a log of some sort.

Having clients keep food logs isn't in and of itself a miracle tool; you, the nutrition coach, need to turn that raw data into something actionable. You have to review the logs. Every two weeks, clients email me their logs or I will take a look at their food logging application, which contains the previous two weeks' worth of daily food intake.

Here's what I look for:

1. Is there an appropriate ratio of protein, carbohydrates and fat?
2. Are the portion sizes appropriate?
3. Is the client eating consistently throughout the day?
4. If something is off, what's the culprit?
5. Are they drinking the recommended amount of water?

I discovered through one client's food logs that she was going over her prescribed fat intake by 20 or more grams each day. Instead of just telling her to reduce her fat intake, which isn't terribly helpful, I helped her find an actionable way to do it. I pointed out that while she was eating a lot of chicken thighs, which is a great source of protein, it was high in fat. By switching to skinless chicken breasts, we could keep her protein up and reduce the extraneous fat. If this client had not been logging her food and simply said she was eating chicken, it would have been hard to make this determination.

Each time I review a log, I give the client three to four pieces of feedback. You want to give actionable advice for your clients to make a change. If they are skipping breakfast, provide a solution that will work for them. If they are overeating snacks, you can recommend a pre-portioned option. Keep it simple to implement. You need to use the data they've given you to ensure your client is on the right track.

Logging doesn't have to be limited to food intake, either. Journaling about everything from energy levels to cravings or even bowel movements can be very instructive for learning how certain foods or macronutrient ratios affect a client's overall well-being. It can also be helpful to track activity levels, whether that means how many fitness classes a client attends per week or how many steps they take in a day.

We all get busy, and life happens. But if we can track our actions, it's going to help us keep our goals a priority.

Accountability Partners

Another important tool is having an accountability partner. While you are absolutely an accountability partner as a nutrition coach, you can't be the only one. Depending on the package the client has purchased, you might only speak with the client once to two times per week. They need additional daily support in between those discussions. The first people your client needs to get on board is their family, and the people in their immediate household.

Take my husband, for instance: He loves cookies. If I was trying to lose weight and he brought cookies home every day, I would eventually give in. Unfortunately, I have seen this scenario play out in the lives of some of my clients. One client worked with me for three years trying to lose weight, but his wife, who was also overweight, wasn't on the same page. It was very tough for him to stay on track because he could never get past the temptations in his own home.

It is not necessarily reasonable to expect everyone in your client's household to adopt the same nutrition plan as your client. Everyone needs to be on the same page with your client's goals and actions steps to help them stay accountable. Your client will be successful if they have the support from the people they are around the most.

Having accountability buddies outside of the household is also incredibly effective. Consider who you spend the most time with during the day. It is most likely your co-workers. If co-workers are pressuring a nutrition client to go out to lunch daily, it can be detrimental to the client's progress. This is where corporate wellness and team challenges evolved, which we will go into more later.

Accountability outside the house can also look like support groups that you help organize among your clients, team nutrition challenges, or group fitness classes. When people become part of a group doing the same things together, they lean on each other during moments of weakness. You can host weekly meetings for support and accountability. Clients might even food prep together or arrange a food swap. Whatever it looks like, it's important that clients have a support system to turn to when they're not meeting with you.

Goal-Setting and Rewards

In Chapter 3, I discussed goal-setting as a part of a client's initial consultation. Goal-setting is also an important on-going component of accountability. The key to making goal-setting an effective tool for accountability is breaking large, long-term goals into smaller, short-term goals.

Consider a common scenario where you have a client whose goal is to lose 50 pounds. Fifty pounds of weight loss is definitely an achievable goal, but if that were her only goal, we'd be setting her up for failure. It's going to take time to lose 50 pounds, and without smaller milestone goals to meet along the way, it would be easy to get frustrated and give up. Along with that 50-pound weight loss goal, we want to specify that she should also lose a certain percentage of body fat. Clients are given reference points for ideal body fat based on healthy standards. If her body fat percentage was 40 percent, we would recommend a reduction of ten to fifteen percent. Then, we break that down into smaller goals of losing one to two pounds per week and one to two percent of body fat per month.

In addition to goal-setting for body fat or weight loss, we want to set action steps for habits. The roadmap to achieving goals is paved through creating healthy habits and action steps. You might have a client who tells you at the point of goal setting that they are only eating two large meals and drinking one cup of water per day. For the first month, their action step would be to increase water intake and have breakfast every day. Combining both goals and actions steps helps clients see it's not just about the number, it is also about the lifestyle changes.

The following month, we would re-evaluate the client's goals. Once the client is comfortable eating more consistently, we could fine-tune that goal to include adding two snacks per day and measure out their food to ensure they are getting adequate macronutrients during meals and snacks. The following month might include a goal for physical activity. As the client progresses month to month, so should their goals and action steps. As client's body fat decreases, their metabolic rate increases. Once clients hit their goals, they are transitioned to a maintenance plan.

A tool to go along with goal-setting is a reward system. We want to steer our clients away from using food as a reward, which can easily lead to a binge. A reward for a client can be a massage or a new pair of shoes. It could be as simple as an hour of alone time, free of responsibilities or obligations. We want people to reward themselves with each short-term goal they meet, but we want those rewards to be compatible with their overall plan for wellness.

Rewards and celebrating successes is an important part of continuing motivation. It works for everyone. I recently wrote an email discussing bouncing back and having a plan to get back on track. You will see it in Chapter 8. It talks about how to get back on track. I have a goal of where I want my body fat percentage to be and two pieces of new athletic clothing in my trunk waiting for me when I reach that goal.

Setbacks

Life happens.

It is not possible to follow a plan perfectly 100 percent of the time. People go on vacations or life deals them a bad hand and it gets tough to stay on track with nutrition. It's important to let your client know it is normal, and they can talk about it with you. In fact, they need to talk about it with you if they want to make a change.

If a client experiences a setback, the first thing I do is listen. I ask them to tell me about the challenges they experienced. Then, even amidst those setbacks, I find a bright spot. We must find those little wins to keep clients motivated. If the conversation is negative the whole time, they're going to feel defeated.

Then, we re-evaluate the client's action steps to address those struggles. We might remove an action step or two. If it turned out that preparing a week's worth of meals was too overwhelming and the client binged on pizza takeout instead, we set a new goal of preparing three meals per week at home. Then, we can select a few restaurants and healthy menu items in advance, so the client has a plan in place for the days he/she doesn't prepare meals at home.

If a client continues to struggle, suggest they increase their package so they can come in for more frequent sessions. We all have setbacks. The question is, how quickly can they bounce back? It is important that your clients move past what happened and get back on track.

The reality of nutrition counseling and coaching is that you have to help your clients adapt their plan when set-backs happen. We recently had a client who signed up for our nutrition program. She was looking for someone to hold her accountable and tell her exactly what she needed to do to be successful with her busy schedule. As the manager of health food stores, she's on the road consistently. Her days started at 4 a.m. and ended with taking her children to ice skating practice at 8 p.m. Clearly, she was exhausted. From this, I could determine that she would not want to prepare meals at night after a long day.

After she left my office, she was excited and motivated to get started with the plan we created. But then some unplanned circumstances took over: Hurricane Irma, specifically. The client was out of power for a few days and it threw off her entire schedule. She came in a few weeks later for a follow-up. She was nervous.

"Nicole, I haven't been to the gym in a month. My nutrition hasn't been the best," she said. I quickly shifted the conversation to focus on what progress she did make over the previous month. Then, she started to share her success from the previous month. She had started making breakfast and she was drinking water in larger quantities. She started preparing lunches instead of eating out every day. She was mindful of what she was putting in her body. Was it perfect? No, but we made some big steps in the right direction. I praised her for the hard work she had done and we made new action steps to work on over the next couple weeks. Your clients need to see the WINS. If they don't, it's your job to point them out.

Prodigal Sons

After launching your nutrition business, you will learn that not everyone will commit to ongoing nutrition coaching. You might have a few clients who aren't ready to commit to a lifestyle change and walk out your door after 30 days. You may even have a client who thinks they learned it all in one month and doesn't need you anymore.

Should you write them off completely? Of course not.

Just as you need a follow-up system in place for active clients, you also need one for inactive clients. I email previous clients after the one- and three-month marks. These emails are not written as a desperate attempt to get them back; they are framed as if they are still a client. I reiterate what their goals were when they first came to see me and ask if they're on track to meet those goals. I ask if they would benefit from some accountability and would like to set up a nutrition appointment.

Another way to reach out is to make sure those clients are on your regular marketing email list. If they're getting your newsletter with nutrition tips and the latest programs and success stories, it's a constant reminder that you're still out there and ready to help them. Just because a client falls off or decides not to continue, that doesn't mean you eliminate them completely from your lists.

Your entire email list, with past and present clients, should be getting something related to nutrition or fitness at least once per week. Part of your roles and tasks as a nutrition coach should be creating the content and scheduling it to be emailed to your entire list. We will revisit content marketing in Chapter 8.

Drawing the Line

As a nutrition coach, you can do a lot for your clients, but you can't make them change if they don't want to. They might say they're ready, but when it comes time to take action, nothing happens.

It doesn't happen often, but when it does, you need to assess your client's readiness to change. If they cancel appointments, aren't following through with the action steps they commit to, or if their food log is inconsistent with the progress, maybe they just aren't ready. Your job as a nutrition coach is to encourage, not reprimand a client.

There is a time and place for being stern but most importantly you need to be compassionate. I once had a client tell me, "I need Mrs. Doubtfire and a Navy Seal in one. Can you be that person for me?"

If a client doesn't implement the goals and action steps you create together, it can be a frustrating process for everyone. At the end of the day, they are only cheating themselves. With that being said, it doesn't mean you are going to continue to waste your time on someone who's not willing to do the work. We have all had a client in the past that we don't like working with because there is always an excuse. They are not part of your perfect day and they shouldn't be. Sometimes, you have to fire a client. The beauty of running your own business is you can!

We talk a lot about building a client base, so discussing firing a client might seem contradictory, however, having the right clients will help you long-term. If you find yourself dreading meeting with a client or if the client is constantly negative and frustrated because they're not seeing results, yet they still don't make the changes you prescribe—those are signs of an uncommitted client. They're not a good fit; they're wasting their money and your time.

Firing clients is tough. In the past five years, I've had to fire three clients for those reasons. At the end of the day, they just weren't ready. There were no hard feelings, and I'll welcome them back when they are ready, but if they're not ready to make a change, there's no point in continuing.

I once worked with a child who was four years old and weighed more than 70 pounds. Both of her parents were doctors. She would only eat macaroni and cheese and pizza. She was considered obese before turning five years old. I sat down with the child and both parents. We started the consult just like every pediatric consult. I let the children talk first, asking them to tell me what they like to do and eat. I'll also ask what foods they would be willing to try, which gives them ownership in the situation.

This child was not willing to try anything. In fact, she threw a temper tantrum in the office because she was refusing to eat anything but the two items listed above. Her mom told her she wouldn't have to try anything and that she could leave the office with the father and play inside the gym. Clearly, the child was in control in this situation.

This child also enrolled in a trial of our CrossFit children class. It went the same way: she refused to participate in anything. I met with the child once or twice after that visit, but nothing changed. The child actually gained weight instead of losing it. Nothing changed at home; portion sizes and food choices remained the same. After a few months of seeing the client, I had a respectful conversation with the mother regarding her progress and we came to the conclusion that it would be best if she did not continue with us. The fact is, this child was not part of my perfect day. I dreaded seeing them because I knew nothing was going to change. The parents weren't ready to reinforce our recommendations at home.

The moral of this story is that if a client isn't ready to make a change—or in this case, if the family isn't ready to make a change—nothing will happen. The client will feel like the program isn't working when in reality there was no action taken outside of the office. I stress the importance of clients taking action during consults. Just because we talk about it, doesn't mean you will see the results you want. Your job is to support, encourage, and give your clients all the tools they need to be successful but that isn't enough for them to see results.

Chapter 5: From Short-Term Challenges to Long-Term Clients

People tend to be inherently competitive, by nature. Because of this, gyms and companies love to implement nutrition challenges. At a private practice, you can use challenges to get in the door of companies you want to partner with for corporate challenges. At a fitness facility, you may have addressed nutrition through challenges in the past. It is easy to assume that a nutrition challenge is enough to get people on a path to good nutrition. In my experience, I have seen many fitness facilities run successful challenges, only to allow members to revert to old habits after it's over.

Challenges are an effective way to kick-start someone's journey to health, as long as there is a plan for when the challenge is over. At HSN, we categorize a challenge as Phase I because it is the first step to a healthy lifestyle and seeing long-term results. Explaining to participants that the challenge is the first step will help them understand those first 20-30 days are just the start. The most important part of the journey comes after the challenge is over in Phase II.

Over 90 percent of the gyms I provide consulting to have run nutrition challenges. Of those 90 percent, the overwhelming majority tell me that as soon as the challenge is over, nutrition is ignored. They know there is a gap in their system because their clients aren't seeing long-term results. Running challenges doesn't provide the structure to help your clients and isn't the solution to having a sustainable nutrition program.

In October 2017, I wrote an article on this topic for the CrossFit Journal called, "The Trap After the Diet Challenge Ends." I recommend that you read the entire article, but this chapter will dive into why it's important to have a nutrition program year-round, not just the 30 to 60 days that you run a challenge.

First, there is a trend for nutrition challenges to promote a specific type of diet that tends to be quite restrictive, like the Paleo or ketogenic diet. Many people can commit to a drastic change in their nutrition when there's an end in sight, but it's unrealistic for the long-term. The goal of a challenge is to help people adopt long-term healthy habits. Short-term goals like dropping 10 pounds are great, but long-term goals and lasting health require a realistic approach that won't send your clients binging after a challenge ends.

Additionally, companies and gyms implement challenges as a stand-alone tool. Participants get excited when the challenge begins, but that excitement wears off after about 30 days. If there is no system in place to hold them accountable to their nutrition goals, clients fall through the cracks and revert to bad habits. Then, they wait for the next challenge—six or more months down the road—to get them back on track.

That doesn't mean nutrition challenges are inherently bad. They are a great way to increase awareness about healthy nutrition habits and kick-start someone's journey within the context of a supportive group of people. Challenges must be implemented as one piece of a larger system geared toward ongoing nutrition support. Challenges will rally your community and provide an initial push to jump start their nutrition. It should be a stepping stone to a more permanent solution.

Timeline for Marketing a Challenge

The gold standard for challenge advertising is four weeks prior to launch. This means you will create infographics, success stories, videos and landing page for the challenge six weeks prior to launch. Part of the income your nutrition coach earns when running a challenge pays for the time it takes to design these marketing tools.

Sample Challenge Infographic:

Timeline to Challenge Launch	Action Required
6 Weeks Out	▪ Create challenge flyer ▪ Create sign-up page through membership portal ▪ Post video talking about the importance of nutrition to achieving your goals ▪ Post infographic "Where is NUTRITION on your priority list?" ▪ Send love letter talking about creating a jumpstart plan for nutrition ▪ Identify challenge sponsors
5 Weeks Out	▪ Create and post video of nutrition coach discussing upcoming challenge and what is included ▪ Send out email regarding challenge ▪ Create event on social medial for challenge kick-off seminar ▪ Post infographic regarding challenge
4 Weeks Out	▪ Post success story with link to sign up ▪ Post infographic of what is included ▪ Discuss upcoming challenge in newsletter ▪ Announce in classes
3 Weeks Out	▪ Send email with sign-up link + success stories ▪ Post video regarding nutrition and developing a plan ▪ If doing a team challenge, make an infographic of each team name and members, then post to social media ▪ Announce in classes
2 Weeks Out	▪ Post video testimonial from past challenge participants ▪ Post success story with link to sign-up ▪ Send two emails discussing challenge with success stories and link to sign-up ▪ Post teams who have signed up ▪ Announce in classes
1 Week Out	▪ Send out "LAST CHANCE" emails with links to sign-up ▪ Announce in classes

Sample Challenge Flyer:

Running A Successful Nutrition Challenge

First, you need to decide the inherent goal and philosophy of the challenge. As I mentioned earlier, steer away from restrictive, dogmatic diets that are unrealistic for long-term adherence. At HSN, the challenges we have designed that are run by gyms all over the world are based on behavior change and creating sustainable healthy habits. We focus on whole foods, hydration, and lifestyle factors like exercise, sleep, and stress relief. To learn more about our challenges, visit **www.healthystepsnutrition.com**.

Then, determine the duration of the challenge. When I first started running challenges, they were 90 days. I found that while people were enthusiastic and committed at the start, the excitement dwindled at around the 30-day mark, even with a challenge rooted in sustainable healthy habits. The 30-day mark is simply the point at which most people will need one-on-one attention and accountability to fine-tune their approach and stay motivated to reach their long-term goals.

Therefore, the gold standard for running nutrition challenges is between 24-30 days. This allows participants to benefit from the group setting then transition to individual coaching. Challenges are designed to convert at least 50 percent of challenge participants to ongoing nutrition counseling or a customized nutrition package after the challenge ends.

Before the challenge officially kicks off, you'll need to get some data from participants. Biometric testing for all participants, before and after the challenge, enables participants to set realistic goals and track their progress over the course of the 28 days. Your clients need to see their hard work paying off; after all, success leads to motivation. We want our clients to be motivated to continue their journey to health. As discussed in Chapter 3, testing a wide range of metrics—body weight, body fat percentage, and physical measurements—will enable clients to understand what they've accomplished beyond the number on the scale.

In order to launch a challenge effectively, create a schedule for biometric testing before the challenge begins. In the past, I've made the mistake of telling participants to simply arrive for testing within a two-hour window before the challenge kick-off presentation. Naturally, everyone showed up 30 minutes before the presentation, and we were scrambling. To stay on schedule, email participants an editable spreadsheet with 15-minute time slots for people to sign up in advance. Advertise the time slots as first come first serve to promote people to sign-up early.

When you're taking participants' physical measurements, it's important to note who's doing the testing for which clients. There will be variation between results if you have different people taking measurements before and after. For example, if I take Mary's measurements at the beginning of the challenge, I need to be the one taking her measurements at the end. If you need additional help during measurements, have someone assist with weight and body fat measurements, rather than physical measurements.

Finally, be consistent with the tool you use to track body fat. Machine results can vary by 1-2% depending on the brand, so changing machines could yield lesser results. A common question I am asked by people looking to launch a challenge is: "Should I rent an X (insert super fancy machine) or a hydrostatic underwater testing machine, such as a dunk tank, for the challenge?" The answer is no. Your clients need consistent measurements after the challenge is over. If you use a dunk tank then transition over to a handheld machine after the challenge is over, their progress tracking isn't accurate. When switching to the handheld machine, their body fat might read 1-2 percent higher. Keep your biometric tools consistent with what you will use during ongoing coaching.

After baseline metrics are completed, it's time for the kick-off seminar. Using a visual presentation as an aid, walk participants through the goals and purpose of the challenge—to establish healthy habits—and dive into some of the details of how to accomplish their goals.

Discuss what macronutrients are and how each affects the body, as well as good sources of those macronutrients. Talk about healthy portion sizes, hydration, and post-workout recovery. After helping gyms run hundreds of challenges all over the world, we know what questions will be asked, as well as the best strategies for success.

Some of the most popular questions we are asked during challenge kickoff seminars include:

- Can I drink coffee?
- What if I use raw sugar cane or agave instead of refined sugar?
- I don't like to eat before I work out, what should I do?
- What is the latest time I should eat before bed?
- When can I have a cheat day?
- What do I do if I'm full and still have more to eat?
- What do I do if I'm still hungry?

The last section of the presentation is goal-setting. Goals drive success, and it's important to set both short- and long-term goals. This is the point you want to drive home throughout the entirety of the challenge: these 28 days are just a jump start. Maybe a client's short-term goal is to lose five pounds over the next four weeks. What's the long-term goal? Maybe it's to lose 50 pounds, prevent disease, or attain certain performance goals in the gym. Goals for the challenge should be stepping stones to those big picture goals.

Challenge goals must be specific. Instead of saying, "I want to lose weight," specify a number. Concrete goals lead to concrete action steps, which lead to success. After the kick-off seminar is done, give the participants homework. They need to go home and post their goals on the challenge social media page. If they are uncomfortable doing that, they need to email the goals privately. Whether it's to the whole group or in an email, a public declaration of goals helps hold participants accountable.

On the same day, email participants a video recapping the kick-off seminar to serve as a reference. Also, post the video in the private challenge social media group.

Challenge participants need resources in addition to what you discuss during the kick-off seminar. The kick-off seminar contains a lot of information and may be overwhelming at first. At HSN, each challenge participant receives a handbook containing more information about the topics discussed, as well as tools like the plate method. We provide tips on topics like food-prepping and how to stay on track while eating out. Additionally, we provide participants with sample meal plans for the length of the challenge and a place for participants to write down their goals.

Once the challenge kicks off, videos and emails are sent to participants weekly discussing different behaviors. These emails include topics like the benefits of choosing whole over processed foods or efficient food-prep techniques.

Sample Email Breakdown:
Week 1: Eat Real Food
Week 2: Drink Up
Week 3: Eating Out and Treats
Week 4: Staying on Track

This information is also posted on the challenge social media groups, which is an important accountability tool in and of itself. The group fosters community engagement and continued accountability, providing a place where participants can share recipes, struggles, successes, and encouragement. In fact, we encourage dietitians and gyms running our program to give people who participate in questions of the day on social media extra points.

The group also provides a platform for you, the nutrition coach, to lead by example. As you follow the challenge nutrition programming yourself, you will post recipes, videos, and words of encouragement in the social media group.

The next step is the accountability piece of the challenge. Each week, the participants are required to turn in their tracking sheet. These sheets, created through an online editable spreadsheet or printed, are part of the resources we provide participants. They contain checkboxes for each day of the week to indicate if they've met their water requirements for the day, completed a workout, followed the meal plan, and participated in a stress-relieving activity. Each box is associated with points. Following the meal plan might be worth three points, whereas stress relief might only be worth one point.

The winner of the challenge must have turned in their tracking sheets. This will ensure your winner actually followed the plan and didn't dramatically restrict calories the last week to achieve the best numbers. The tracking sheets serve two purposes: to hold participants accountable to the plan and to give us more data to refer to at the end of the challenge when we retest biometrics and set new goals.

With ongoing nutrition coaching clients, the gold standard to review their food logs weekly or biweekly. This is a perk of becoming an ongoing coaching client. During the challenge, clients log their food but we don't review it like we do with ongoing coaching clients. Of course, you can choose to review anyone's food log if they request it throughout the challenge, but it isn't required. After all, we know that if clients log their food, they are more likely to be successful with achieving goals. We want people to get into the habits of meal prepping, eating around workouts, drinking water, cutting out the processed food, and getting enough sleep.

After the second set of biometrics are taken at the end of the challenge, the winner is determined based on the percentages rather than raw numbers. For instance, if Matt lost 15 pounds but only 2 percent of his body weight and Suzie lost 10 pounds but 6 percent of her body weight, she should be the winner. Winners should be based around weight, body fat, inches, and behaviors. Celebrate the participants who made positive lifestyle changes. Prizes could range from a free month of ongoing nutrition counseling to a free personal training session, or even a goodie bag with protein supplements and workout gear.

..ngagement During the Challenge

Last year, we added a contest in the first two weeks of the challenge for social media engagement. The participant who posted the most pictures of meal prepping, healthy foods, snack ideas, new recipes and used the hashtag #healthystepsnutrition on social media posts won the contest. We also do another contest for checking into the gym. The winners might get a shirt, but it's about building awareness for the brand. We will talk about the power of social media in a later chapter.

After the Challenge

Remember that dismal statistic that 97 percent of people who lose weight don't keep it off? Your job is to ensure your clients don't become one of those statistics.

When I schedule challenge participants for post-challenge biometric testing, I allot 20 minutes per person. We will update their biometrics and talk about how the challenge went. We discuss:

- What were their bright spots/successes?
- What did they struggle with?
- Did they achieve their goal?

- What's their next goal?

Log this information to refer to at a later time. Writing it down on the back of the biometric testing sheet allows for easy access.

Whether clients met their goals or not during the challenge is almost irrelevant; both circumstances provide a window to ongoing nutrition counseling. If they met their short-term goal of losing 10 pounds, re-evaluate their goals and discuss how ongoing nutrition counseling and a more customized plan can help them lose their next 10, and the 10 after that. If they hit a little bump in the road on week three, they will need your help to get back on track. Of course, ongoing nutrition counseling can afford them the greater level of accountability that they need.

If challenge participants know there's another follow-up nutrition visit scheduled, they will stick with the healthy habits they built over the previous 28 days. They won't be celebrating the challenge's end by eating an entire pizza and pitcher of beer.

Your clients will realize the value of continuing their journey with one-on-one nutrition counseling. But even if they decide to hold off on signing up for ongoing coaching right away, that doesn't mean you shouldn't continue to reach out to them. Use your notes to send a follow-up email reminding your client of all the awesome progress they made during the challenge. You also want to help them find a solution to the struggles they had during the challenge. Then, end the check-in email with a link to book an on-going coaching session. There are many times we have had people come back and sign up for ongoing coaching after they realize it's tough to stick with it on your own.

Charging for Challenges

Many gyms and facilities run nutrition challenges for free. As a RD looking to open a private practice, you need to charge to run challenges at fitness facilities or companies. As a gym owner, you can also charge participants for nutrition challenges. You are providing a service that will lead them to results, so treat it as such. Gyms that are a part of the HSN affiliate consulting program charge anywhere between $89 and $119 per person for participation in nutrition challenges.

We have found that if you do not value the service you are providing with a cost, your clients will not be invested in the process. Challenges provide support to kick-start your participants' journeys to health. You are spending time working with these clients to help them achieve their goals. Challenges lay the ground work by providing nutrition education to clients and start them on a plan to make a lifestyle change, this is why we equate a challenge as part of Phase I.

Chapter 6: The Right Fit to Run Your Program & Compensation

Once you've determined the philosophy and phase structure of your nutrition program, it's time to decide who will run it. Earlier in the book, I explained two ways to bring expertise and authority to your program: become an expert or hire one.

The first option is executing the nutrition program yourself, whether that means you run the day to day or delegate it to a member on your staff. If you are a RD looking to open a practice, you will be taking on the majority of the day to day operations as well as growth strategies. At some point, you will need to hire staff to take your practice to the next level.

The second option is to partner with someone who owns a private practice. Partnering with someone who is established will increase credibility of your program. There could be some potential conflicts of interest if partnering with someone who owns a practice. If you still choose this route, you must define the partnership clearly and ensure the person you partner with will be invested in promoting your program, not their private practice. Depending on the goals for your business, having a partnership might still be the right choice.

Where Are You Getting Your Information From?

Registered Dietitian	VS	Nutritionist
• Licensed • Must Pass A Board Exam • Undergraduate Degree in Nutrition • Internship Requiring 1200+ Hours of Supervised Practice • Required Ongoing Continuing Education		• Not A Legally Backed Term • Anyone Can Call Themselves A Nutritionist • May Have Taken A Weekend Online Course • Not Qualified To Treat Disease

Do Your Research Before Implementing Your Program.

Partnering with an established RD is a solution if you don't have a good fit to run a nutrition program and don't have time to do it yourself. Another reason to partner with a RD is if you are looking to provide more comprehensive services for your community such as medical nutrition therapy and customized meal plans. Setting up a partnership with a RD would allow for quicker implementation and save you time with creating the resources needed for a successful nutrition program.

If you choose to partner, do your research when searching for the right fit. Anyone can identify themselves as a nutritionist; becoming "certified" is only a two-hour course online. Many people refer to themselves as a nutrition expert but it's important to know what you should look for. Registered dietitians must complete a bachelor's degree and an internship which includes over 1200 hours of supervised practice before taking a board exam. Most states require a candidate to be a registered dietitian prior to applying for licensure. For instance, in Florida, I need both my RD and LDN status to be active to practice. They are renewed separately every five and two years respectively.

Most states also have laws prohibiting anyone other than an RD from writing meal plans for clients. If you want to provide that level of customization, or provide nutritional advice to anyone with a medical condition, you'll need to partner with a RD. If you partner with a nutritionist and someone becomes sick, it is a liability to your business.

You can find out more about your state requirements here: **https://www.cdrnet.org/state-licensure** or **http://www.nutritionadvocacy.org/laws-state**.

Choosing a Partner

The key quality to consider when evaluating a potential partner in your nutrition venture is: *Are this person's values consistent with what we teach?* Use these indicators to determine an appropriate partnership.

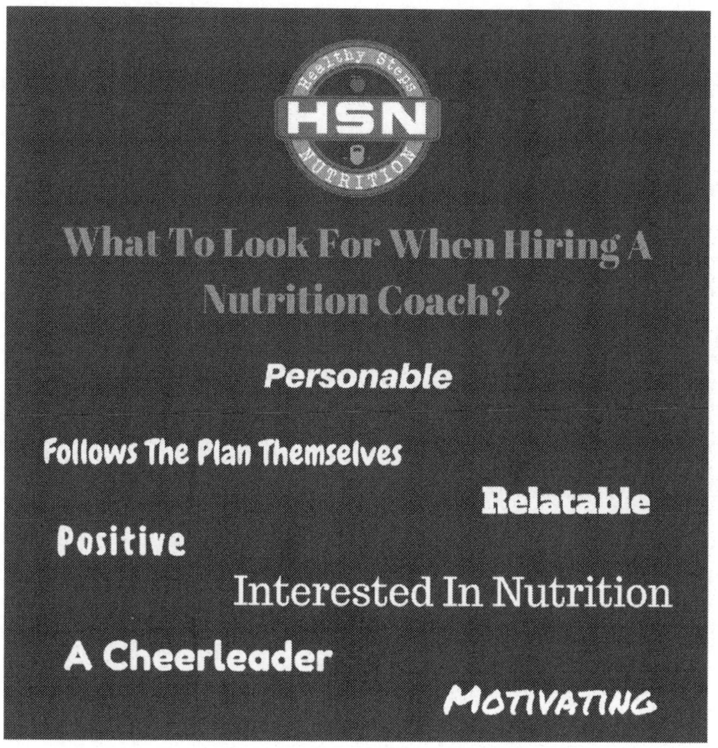

- ***They communicate your message.***

  If your vision for a nutrition program focuses on balance and whole foods, your partner should not be part of a multi-level marketing scheme that pushes protein supplements and pills; this would conflict with your message. Ensure that the program your partner prescribes is consistent with the message you want to convey to your potential clients.

- ***They follow your philosophy.***

In addition to communicating the message of your nutrition program effectively, anyone associated with your business also needs to follow the philosophy. If your nutrition coach or partner tells your clients to stay away from doughnuts and ice cream, but posts a picture eating a box of Bavarian Creams, how much will that impact their credibility, and as a result, the credibility of the entire program? A client will think that they can do the same.

- ***They are a professional "bright spot" engineer.***

Your program leader also needs to have a persona conducive to the job. In April 2016, I replaced myself as the dietitian in my own program at CrossFit HSN in order to focus on developing HSN Consulting. When I was looking for someone to run the program, I looked for a cheerleader. Someone who was positive, friendly, engaging, and motivating.

Your nutrition coach needs to be able to find what Chris Cooper, founder of Two-Brain Business, calls “bright spots.” These are the actions a client is doing well. Maybe your client eats ice cream every night, but also drinks eight glasses of water per day. An effective nutrition coach will recommend the client reduce the ice cream intake, of course, but a cheerleader will celebrate the client for good hydration.

- ***They are a go-getter.***

Finally, you need someone who is a go-getter. Clients will not fly through your door. You have to promote it. Your nutrition coach or business partner must actively promote your program through content, highlight people doing well, and provide your program with a face. This might be the toughest hat to wear but the most important when it comes to growing a program and building your brand.

The outlined roles and tasks clarify and reinforce the responsibilities of a nutrition coach outside of client meetings. Anyone running the HSN program discusses these tasks with their potential nutrition coach before appointing them to run the program. Consider this situation: A gym owner appointed someone to be the nutrition coach. This person was very interested and knowledgeable about nutrition and followed a balanced nutrition plan as well. It was a perfect fit; right?

Once the nutrition coach started running the program, however, the person was asked to complete some roles and tasks that they were not comfortable completing, such as creating content and posting regularly on social media. The person knew a lot about nutrition but wasn't the "face" of the program and didn't talk to members about their nutrition.

After a few months of an unsuccessful launch, the owner took the program back over and went on a search for the right fit. This time, the owner clearly discussed the roles and responsibilities so both parties were on the same page. Once they found the right person, the program grew exponentially.

The new nutrition coach created content weekly and implemented "No Snack Intros," which we will go over in the next chapter. In fact, they now convert 9 out of 10 clients who come in for a free 15-minute nutrition session to nutrition clients. This demonstrates how the perfect fit means the difference between a profitable program and a program that does not get off the ground.

Once you identify a partner or good fit to run your program using the above criteria, determine their level of presence within the facility. You want members and the community to respect them as the expert. *In order to be successful, your nutrition coach or partner must have an active presence in your community.* They must care about all clients. Among the gyms that run our nutrition program, there is a direct correlation between having an active program leader and the growth of the program.

Don't underestimate the importance of an active presence. When setting up a partnership, clearly define your expectations if you are bringing someone from the outside to work with your clients.

Here are some considerations if partnering with someone who owns a nutrition business:

- How often will they provide you content? Will the content include their business name?
- If they own a private practice, clearly define the relationship. Will they discuss their own private practice with your nutrition clients?
- Are they corresponding with your clients via an email address under your umbrella or their own business?
- Where are they meeting with your clients?
- If you own a gym, will they be active at your facility?
- Will materials given to clients have your logo on them or be branded with their business?

Your members and clients respect you. If you put your name behind a person, service, or product, it must be something you would do yourself or recommend to your family. I recently had a gym who was interested in running our program. They paid to have one of their members work with me individually first. The member learned more about the client experience and gave feedback to see if our program was a good fit for them to run at their facility.

When considering a partnership with a local RD, ask for client feedback or work with them yourself to see if it would be a good fit with your business model.

In whatever partnership you choose to develop, the gold standard is to seek out partners who are outside of a 20-mile radius from your own private practice or fitness facility. At HSN, our employees and dietitian sign a non-compete clause and agree not to operate their own private practice within that 20-mile radius. Initially this might turn away potential partners, but in the long run, it will safeguard your business.

Branding Your Nutrition Program

Naming your program is a nerve-wracking first step for a business owner. For us, it was simple. Healthy Steps Nutrition came first, and CrossFit HSN fit perfectly under the original umbrella. If you are a RD looking to start a private practice, you want your name to be clear, easily recognizable, and easy to remember. Your name sets the precedent for what will happen at your facility.

For gym owners, if your gym is called Fitness123 but the nutrition program is called Clean Eating Nutrition, it will be tough for clients to connect the two. People following your content need to easily recognize that you offer both services. That's exactly what Brian Alexander, owner of CrossFit Illumine, now Illumine Nutrition & Fitness, did in 2017. He's rebranded to be seen as THE place for nutrition and fitness.

Here is where partnering with an outside RD with an established practice will cause a conflict. As a dietitian, I want exposure for my brand. As the owner of a gym, I want the nutrition program's brand to be consistent with my primary brand. When I hired the RD to take over for me, she had a new private practice. She did not post anything on our social media pages about her private practice; no one even knew she had a private practice. All the work she did and clients she saw at our gym were under the HSN umbrella.

Of course, if these options do not fit in your plan—building a nutrition program from scratch, starting your own private practice, or partnering with a dietitian—you can opt to get your resources and process from a dietitian with an established program and appoint a person to implement the program. That's what we provide at HSN.

Dietitians and gym owners who sign up for the HSN Consulting Program receive a turn-key nutrition program. The appointed nutrition coach and owner complete a detailed and structured online course to learn the fundamentals of implementing a nutrition program. After completing the training process, they receive a ready-to-launch package.

The HSN Consulting Package Includes:

- Online course
- Training completion call
- Website landing page template
- Social media release template
- Handbooks and client resources
- Meal plans
- Client meeting structure
- Marketing materials
- Success stories
- Video content
- Content marketing via email
- Consult forms
- Tracking tools
- Blogs
- Nutrition tips
- Monthly mentoring calls
- Continuing education webinars
- Access to a private social media group
- Email access
- Ongoing support

With this model, you focus on running your business. You do not spend countless up-front hours creating a system that has already been proven to work.

HSN Consulting has helped hundreds of gym owners and dietitians implement nutrition programs. They not only receive all the materials they need to implement a successful program; they also participate in monthly mentoring calls to help grow their programs. They have access to a bank of nutrition resources and content that is constantly updated. HSN Consulting clients have an online portal for client management. Finally, they are members of a private group on social media where they can bounce ideas off of the other hundreds of people running the program.

I have heard fellow dietitians say countless times that they don't have time to create the resources they need to run a successful private practice. Gym owners know nutrition is important, but many don't have the credentials or confidence to implement a nutrition program on their own. They need guidance with setting up, structuring, and launching a nutrition program. Just as nutrition clients need accountability, so do nutrition programs. HSN Consulting provides RDs and gym owners with a turn-key solution to start a private practice or add nutrition programs. We've helped RDs and gym owners create a steady revenue stream through nutrition programming.

This book is the first step to learning how to implement a nutrition program. If you are looking for more help, you can download free resources and a webinar on the website, **https://healthystepsnutrition.com/nourish/**.

Adding Staff

At some point, you won't be able to add more nutrition clients to your plate and effectively serve them. You're presented with opportunities, but you can't take them on because you have too many personal clients. As you grow, you will need help. If you are the only person seeing clients, it does not provide you the time to grow your business. Time becomes the limiting factor.

At any given moment at HSN, we might have four to five projects in addition to local and distance clients. For instance, in November 2017, we ran a corporate challenge, launched a second one at the company's sister facility, presented a seminar series at a local gymnastics facility, and taught a week-long nutrition education series at a private school, in addition to our local and distance nutrition clients. We were also following up with leads for other large-scale nutrition programs.

Two years ago, I would have done it alone and wouldn't have executed everything very well. At a certain point, I realized that I had to hire a team to execute projects. Having a system will ensure that when you are ready to expand, you are able to do so. It starts with a playbook; write down what you do and how you do it, so when it comes time to hire, you can transfer the knowledge.

This also goes back to consistency. If a nutrition client sees you for a consult, they must have the same experience if their next meeting is with another member of your team.

At the beginning, it is challenging to think ahead to the point where you need to train someone to see clients, but documenting your system now saves time. Adding staff will give you more time to set up partnerships, to market, and to grow your program.

Here is how knowledge is transferred to new employees at HSN:

1. The new staff member completes the online course that every dietitian and nutrition coach running our program must complete before running the program.

2. The new staff member will shadow me during four different initial nutrition consultations and three follow-up/on-going coaching sessions. We discuss my thought process with each consultation and why the actions steps/customized plan were designed that way. We review the notes and draft the follow-up emails to the client.

3. The new staff member leads three initial consultations with me present. I provide feedback and help fill in the gaps when necessary. We discuss the next steps and what is expected after the client left the office. I review the notes and we discuss what to include in the notes to be used as a reference later. The new staff member will draft and schedule the follow-up emails.

4. We shoot video content. The new staff member will write nutrition blogs and tips to establish expertise.

5. We post success stories of the nutrition clients that work with the new staff member.

Compensation for Nutrition Coaches

At HSN, the payment structure is simple. We follow the four-ninths model, wherein the nutrition coach receives 44.4 percent of the nutrition program. Here is the full breakdown of where all the money goes:

4/9: Nutrition coach payment

2/9: Operating expenses for the facility

3/9: Profit for the gym or facility to expand and grow

Here is another way to look at it:

$$$$$$$$$: “Here's all the money.”
$$$$: "Coach, here's what you'll get."
$$: "This pays for the rent, power, and insurance for us to run this place.”
$$$: "This is for the gym. It'll allow the gym to profit from the program, purchase equipment, and continue to grow."

With this successful model, coaches can make more money depending on the number of clients they schedule. It gives them motivation to grow. In a private practice where you are running the program yourself, 4/9 is what you pay yourself as the lead of the program.

The model benefits the person running the program. Consider a dietitian working at a standard hospital job. They make a set wage regardless of how many hours they work. There’s no possibility of increasing their income without a raise.

With the four-ninths model, there is no cap on earning potential. Whereas a dietician employed in a hospital might make $250 in a day, a successful nutrition coach might make $70 in an hour. As someone with over eight years of experience in the healthcare industry, that is a motivational factor.

Choosing the right fit for your nutrition program is a strategic process. In a private practice, you will eventually hire someone to replace yourself as the business grows. If you rush to choose a person that is not the appropriate fit, you risk spending a lot of time, money, and effort on a program that will not be appropriately fostered.

Chapter 7: Marketing Your Program

Off the top of your head, you can likely name at least ten pills, shakes, or products that claim quick weight loss. Products and FADs continue to sell despite the lack of research backing them. Obviously, something is working for these companies in the area of marketing, and it probably isn't the lasting results of their users. Effective marketing will define the growth and long-term success of a program.

Marketing Platforms

Multilevel marketing companies and "pop-up" businesses rely on a platform that continually bombards their target market. It is a platform that reaches audiences the moment they open their eyes, during their commute, on their lunch break, and every second of their day until they fall asleep. They target users through phones cradled in hand.

A study conducted by Flurry shows U.S. consumers spend more than five hours a day on mobile devices. About 86 percent of that time is spent on smartphones. Therefore, we spend about four hours and 15 minutes on our mobile phones every day.[11]

So how do we get in front of our target audience for just a portion of that time? One successful platform is social media. Social media is a highly effective way to build awareness about your brand, authority, and credibility.

We all firmly believe our services will speak for themselves. The results your clients will see by meeting with you every month, following your carefully designed nutrition plan, and exercising regularly, are undoubtedly going to be better than what they'll get from pills, shakes, and wraps. However, you have to get those clients through the door first. Unless your social media presence is as strong or stronger than the programs you're competing with, no one will know you have a door to walk through.

When we first launched the consulting program, I didn't stress the importance of using social media to the extent that we do now. Gyms would run a challenge with 50-60 people and never post one success story or anything related to nutrition on their social media. If you aren't talking about nutrition, how are your members or people in the community going to know that you offer nutrition services beyond just a challenge?

Social media isn't the only platform for marketing a nutrition program. Take a moment to search online for the word "nutritionist" in your city. When I did this search for Boca Raton, the first website was a directory of dietitians and nutrition experts. When I started my practice, I signed up to have my name listed on that site. Some of my most loyal nutrition clients have come from that site. Over five years later, I'm still active on that directory. If you are a new RD, sign up for the first directory site that appears on your online search.

After years of being established, our largest referral sources come from past clients, our partnerships, and email content. However, until you have current clients, you will need a source of referrals. A nutritionist directory is a strong starting point.

No-Snack Intro

When a potential client is ready to take the next step, you need an easy way for them to access you or your nutrition coach. Facilities using our program set up a No-Snack Intro, a name developed by Jeff Burlingame. This intro is a free 15-minute consultation for people who are interested in nutrition services. At a new private practice, this is a way you can meet potential clients.

The No-Snack Intro bridges the gap between an informal conversation and commitment to a nutrition program.

During the intro, you will determine what your clients are doing now, what they have done in the past, and what motivated them to come to you to make a change. At the end of the consult, they must come to the conclusion that they need you to help. Clients should walk away from the No Snack Intro with resources. Dietitians and gyms using the HSN program provide No-Sweat Intro consultations with the *Introduction to Nutrition Handbook*. The handbook provides some basic tips and guidance to make positive changes.

Advertising a No-Snack Intro or a free 15-minute consultation to familiarize yourself with potential nutrition clients creates a path from interest to action. Nutrition coaches who actively implement the No-Snack Intro through HSN convert on average over 75 percent of people who book this free consultation to paying clients. In a private practice, you will convert an even larger number because they are coming to you only for nutrition.

Sample No-Snack Intro Post:

Deciding What to Post

Running a personal social media account versus a business account is very different, and requires thought and discretion. If you've never run a social media account for a business, brainstorming items to post will be overwhelming.

Instead of approaching your nutrition program's social media accounts as a vast void that needs special content, treat it like you would a client. The content HSN posts falls into one of three main categories:

Answers to common questions or problems

If one client has a question, there are more people with the same question. You do not want clients to look for the answer online; you want to provide them the resources to answer their questions. Take the most commonly asked questions and post your responses. If you are creating content regarding what people have questions about, you will build a following.

Here are some of the most popular social media posts that developed from commonly asked questions:

- What should I eat after my work out?
- How can I improve the performance of my teen athlete?
- What tools are the best for meal prepping?
- What is the best snack bar?

- What should I do if I don't like breakfast?
- How can I drink more water?
- How can I get my child to eat vegetables?

Consider the different avenues you might use to answer these questions. You can post two different videos, an infographic, a plain text post, a blog, and a picture with a caption. If you only do one type of post, you are missing out on a group of people who don't follow or might not watch that media type.

Recipes

Think about where you commonly search for recipes in today's society. Cookbooks are gathering dust while you look on the internet for a new recipe. You might even share viral recipes on social media, or post your own perfected recipe.

The recipe page on our website is the most viewed page. People are constantly checking for recipes we have added. When we add a recipe, we post a picture with a link to our website that includes ingredients, nutrition facts, and directions. Wherever you post recipes, link back to your website. By drawing more traffic to your website, you will increase your rank on search engines, and if you have a pixel set up (we will talk about that in a little bit), you can target those people for advertisements.

Sample Recipe Post:

Success Stories

I can't overstate how important success stories are. People will explore your social media pages who have not committed to nutrition coaching. They want inspiration. They're looking for a success story to make them feel like they can be successful, too.

It is important to share more than a simple before-and-after photo comparison. In fact, before and after photos are not compelling—especially in the context of a short-term nutrition challenge.

You are limiting success to what people might perceive in an image. At HSN, our clients create highlight boards. These boards are a visual representation of the health and wellness goals clients met. We take pictures of clients in front of their boards and write a short summary to accompany the image. Instead of saying "Veronica lost five pounds," our success stories might look like, "Veronica successfully eliminated added sugar from her diet for 30 days, achieved her first pull-up, lost 5 pounds, and lost one percent body fat!"

Highlight Board Examples:

"Meet Kar! He decided to take his healthy eating to the next level the past two months. He switched from a meal delivery service to following a customized meal plan we designed for him. Not only did he lose fat but his cholesterol improved by over 100 POINTS! Way to go, Kar!" #healthystepsnutrition #guidedtestedproven

"Meet Miguel! He has worked so far being consistent with the gym and his eating despite a busy work schedule. We are so proud of all his hard work eating healthy and pushing during classes. Awesome job, Miguel!" #healthystepsnutrition #guidedtestedproven

As you can see, the highlight boards are comprehensive as far as lifestyle changes, in addition to physical changes.

The three types of posts discussed above are only a sampling of the possibilities for social media. You will also post about food prep, goal-setting, and how to read nutrition labels. You can also recycle content in various media types.

For every message you create, you should repeat it 10 times in 10 different ways. People process information differently; some read blog posts, while others prefer videos. Some will only click if there's a picture. If you only post written recipes, you're alienating a portion of your potential audience. Recycle a recipe post by making a video instead, or recycle a post about how much sugar is in a juice box with a visual representation of that sugar.

Eventually, you will search your archives and copy yourself. When I first started, I made a video about three-compartment containers and how they illustrate a healthy ratio of protein, carbohydrates and fat in a meal. It was viewed about 8,000 times, and if it was popular a year ago, it will be even more popular now. I could make a new version of the same video, saying the same things in a different way or in a different setting.

Regardless of the content you produce, always link back to your website. You want people to associate your content with your brand and easily access your packages and registration. Your job is to help sort fiction from facts and educate your clients to make healthy lifestyle choices rather than jumping to the next FAD diet.

While the majority of your content should be helping, not selling, it is important that your audience is aware of how you can help them beyond the free nutrition tips and posts. You want to bridge the gap, explain how you are different, and how you can help.

Sample Social Media Post About the Next Step:

Social Media Tools

Running social media is a full-time job. As a business owner, you will employ some tools to increase efficiency.

There are numerous applications and programs that act as a central hub for social media. You will use them to craft and schedule multiple messages to be sent to multiple social media platforms at various times. At HSN, I use an application that generates an image of our logo with each post. We schedule posts to go out through this application for various social media platforms.

Social media platforms also have marketing tools available for business accounts. On Facebook, for example, you can target certain demographics by paying to "boost" a post toward an audience with a particular interest using a key word.

It's important to be specific with this. Boosting a post with the keyword "nutrition" is going to target such a broad audience that you're unlikely to reach an audience that is actually interested in what you offer. I find it effective to target posts towards people who've already liked my social media pages or visited our website. They've already shown an initial interest, and are therefore more likely to consider using HSN in the future.

To track website visitors, we use Facebook Pixel. A pixel acts as a metaphorical camera, which, when installed on your website, uses cookies to track who visits your website and what they do there. That data is used to create targeted Facebook ads for those visitors. Installing pixels on your website increases your presence in the social media feeds of your followers.

Finally, focus on analytics. Behind the scenes of any business's social media page is a host of numbers indicating the posts receiving the most hits. This is your feedback machine; if you're posting mostly pictures but your analytics show that videos get more hits per post, adjust your strategy.

How Much—and When—To Post

One thoughtfully crafted post per day can have a big impact. The key with social media is to be consistent. Avoid posting multiple posts early in the week, and then not posting anything in the latter half of the week. Consistent, high-quality content will earn the respect of your followers.

I schedule all of my posts for the week on Sunday night, timing them to publish in the morning because morning posts are less likely to get lost in the newsfeed. To ensure I'm offering a variety of posts, each day is dedicated to a different topic. You can do this by making a calendar for your social media posts.

Sample Social Media Calendar:

Monday	Mobility minutes
Tuesday	Testimonial or client story (nutrition related)
Wednesday	Fun with fitness
Thursday	Athlete picture
Friday	Food for thought/nutrition video
Saturday	Anything goes
Sunday	Personal records board

Our CrossFit and nutrition business share the same social media channels. We highlight all of our services. By keeping the pages together, we are building our brand as both the fitness and nutrition experts.

If you are a RD and don't offer fitness at your practice, you can schedule your social media content as follows:

Monday	Motivational minutes- tips to help your clients stay on track
Tuesday	Nutrition client success story
Wednesday	
Thursday	Share a social media post from a nutrition client
Friday	Food for thought/nutrition video

Saturday	
Sunday	Healthy Recipe

When you schedule your posts in advance, you still need to monitor your social media accounts. When someone posts a comment, you need to respond. The more interaction your page receives, the more it will appear in people's newsfeeds. The purpose of social media is to build relationships with your followers.

Reviews

The internet isn't always a friendly place, and with all the opportunity and potential social media has to offer comes the risk that someone will use it to try to hurt your business. I challenge you to find one company without at least one negative review.

So, what should you do if someone posts a negative review on your social media page? Most business social media pages will not allow you to delete reviews, but even if you could, don't. Instead, respond positively to the review as quickly as possible. Ask questions to find out why this person had a negative experience, apologize if necessary, and offer a solution. If you start attacking someone on your social media page, it does not reflect well on you or your business. Don't let emotions override professionalism.

For as much as it seems like a bad review might harm you, a good review can have a large positive impact. Consider what you do when you're looking for a new product or service. You ask friends for recommendations and read other customers' product reviews online. In a sea of positive reviews, one negative one will be dismissed as the outlier it is.

You can get more reviews by asking for them, even if it makes you uncomfortable. Someone might love your program, but not think to write a review unless you ask. One activity we implemented at CrossFit HSN is a bingo game with clients, which included nutrition activities. Instead of letters or numbers, the squares on the bingo card are tasks, such as "post a healthy recipe to the social media group," or "review HSN on search engines." Members received a special edition shirt if they finished the entire card.

If you are looking for more reviews, you need to ask your clients individually to write one. If you ask a roomful of people, not many will take action. If you approach a specific client individually, it will often yield a better result. You can say: "John, you've done such a great job increasing your water intake and reducing your sugar intake. Your hard work is really paying off! We'd love it if you would consider sharing your story and writing a review for us on social media."

Organic interaction on social media means more than advertising. If people share your posts or talk about you on social media in a positive way, you'll reach clients you otherwise never would have.

Delegate

Social media marketing can be a daunting task. If you are not comfortable taking on this task, hire a professional or student to do it for you.

You don't need a big budget and someone with a marketing degree to have a successful social media campaign. Hire an intern at $10-15 an hour for a couple hours a week, or hire a client who has shown interest in helping.

If you are social media savvy, you can still delegate these tasks due to time constraints. As a dietitian or gym owner, you need to look at the value of your time, and you might not have the time to worry about the next tweet or what caption to write beneath a photo.

At HSN, our General Manager is responsible for the majority of the posts. Managing social media is a lower level task that can easily be handed to someone else as long as branding stays consistent. You don't have to do everything. And, if you want everything done well, you probably shouldn't.

Chapter 8: Creating Content

The programs we offer at HSN grow and evolve all the time. We offer solutions to our client's biggest challenges. Providing resources for clients to get started with solving these issues is one of the most valuable resources you can provide to them.

Email Marketing

Creating content through social media, email, and newsletters is critical to establishing your expertise. Creating content is the gold standard for building organic awareness and interest about your programs. We spend countless hours each month creating content that is provided for free to people who have expressed interest in our services or are following portals.

It wasn't until 2016 that I started utilizing the hundreds of emails we have on our email list. Prior to that, I sent out a newsletter once every six months. I was missing out. I did not realize the value of content marketing until I was challenged to create content for 30 days. My mentor challenged me to write daily to our email list. I answered the questions we get asked often. No sales pitch, just tips to help or stories that would relate to people.

These "love letters" to clients are one of the most successful marketing tools we have implemented to target clients who are on the fence. When brainstorming topics for love letters, write down questions that you get asked often. Give clients the answers.

Our most popular love letter was personal. I shared how I stopped focusing on nutrition while redoing our house and gutting our kitchen. Then I shared my action plan of getting back on track.

Sample Love Letter

Subject line: Can you bounce back?

"We have all been there. We make every effort to make nutrition and fitness a priority, then "life happens." You get busy and all of a sudden, your good habits of meal prepping and setting yourself up for success are gone. You feel like you can never get back on track. So, how do you snap out of it? For most of us, we see a picture and can't believe it. Maybe we had stopped getting on the scale because we didn't want to face the reality, and when we step back on, we are shocked.

For me, it was a picture from over the weekend. As a dietitian and owner of a CrossFit, my body is my business card. I am a firm believer in practicing what I preach, but life happened to me. The past few months have been crazy. With the business requiring more time, writing a book, a move, and house renovation, meal prepping was impossible. Literally, impossible. In fact, we did not have a functioning kitchen until last week.

Because of this, we've eaten out almost every meal for the past two months. While we try to eat healthy, we have no control over the preparation methods or portion sizes on our plate. Over time, it all adds up.

But now, the kitchen is ready and my excuses are gone. It's time to bounce back. Meal prepping started and lunches are prepped. Snacks are packed and healthy breakfast options are prepared. No matter how hard you work in the gym, you can't out-exercise a diet of eating out.

We all have our struggles. How you bounce back dictates how that chapter of your story ends. Maybe it's a couple months off track, maybe it's a year or two. No matter how long it's been, it's never too late.

Find yourself an accountability partner, come up with a plan, and stick with it. The best advice we can give anyone is to get started doing something that will result in a healthy lifestyle. Maybe that means cutting out the soda, juice, and diet drinks and increasing water consumption. Maybe it looks like bringing your lunch or cutting out the fried foods. Maybe it looks like doubling your vegetable intake with every meal. Whatever it is, make a step today to help you achieve your goals.

I'm getting on our InBody scanner tomorrow morning to find out what my current biometrics are. It's time to track progress to ensure I'm achieving my goals.

What are you going to do to achieve your health and fitness goals?

Take action!

Love, Nicole

This love letter prompted five former fitness clients to reach out and sign up for our fitness services. It also prompted one person to sign up for nutrition services. The goal of this love letter wasn't written to get clients, it was to be honest. We are all human and all fall off the wagon. Clearly, the message hit home.

Once you write your love letter and send it to your email list, share it to your blog and social media accounts. This will expand the reach of your content.

Newsletters

Providing content in a newsletter is another path to increasing expertise, visibility, and providing free help. Accountability is the most important part when achieving and maintaining weight loss goals; content will support with accountability.

Deciding what to discuss in the nutrition education component of your newsletter depends on what your clients need at that moment. For example, during the holidays, include nutrition tips for surviving the holidays and healthy holiday recipes. During the summer, include tips to stay hydrated and some refreshing snack recipes.

Be consistent with your newsletters. Start by sending them out every two months, then move to monthly. The gold standard for newsletters is monthly updates.

HSN Newsletter Components:

1. Highlight events over the past month
2. Client success story - highlight a nutrition client
3. Any program updates
4. Nutrition tip (content)
5. Recipe of the month

Newsletters and email content need to be on your schedule of tasks each month to build awareness of your brand and the nutrition services you offer. Have a clear and consistent intent with every post.

In 2017, we implemented a content schedule to help with consistency. Our viewers get something from Healthy Steps Nutrition & CrossFit HSN at least once per week. You want to stay in the forefront of people's minds so when they are ready to take action, your brand is the first place they go for help.

Sample Email Monthly Schedule:

Day 5: Monthly newsletter with a nutrition success story, listing nutrition hours and a recipe of the month
Day 10: Nutrition love letter
Day 14: Nutrition love letter
Day 20: Nutrition love letter
Day 24: Nutrition tips and a healthy recipe

The goal is to build the email list of people who are interested. You will have a few people who will unsubscribe from your email list because you are putting out so much content. Most likely, they weren't going to sign up for your services anyway.

When we talk to RDs and affiliate owners, time is often the limiting factor when it comes to producing content. This is why we provide affiliates and RDs running HSN Consulting with two nutrition love letters, recipes and weekly nutrition tips to post each month. They no longer need to spend the time creating nutrition content, all they need to do is post it to their platform.

Writing for Magazines & Journals

At HSN, we started writing for reputable websites and magazines to provide resources for the community and build awareness of our brand.

For example, we were hired by the CrossFit Journal to write a series of articles discussing how fitness facilities can implement successful nutrition programs. This exponentially increased our reach. Once posted, we shared the articles we wrote for the CrossFit Journal and other health magazines with our email list, social media, and on our website. They became part of a drip campaign for anyone interested in running our consulting program.

Here is the list of topics we addressed in the CrossFit Journal:

1. Nutrition Beyond the Challenge
2. Valuing Your Time
3. Hiring the Right Fit to Run Your Nutrition Program
4. Building Ongoing Coaching
5. Systemizing a Nutrition Program
6. Providing Nutrition Content

I set aside the first hour of my morning to write content. Don't be afraid to talk about the same topic in different ways. You will write a love letter, make a video for social media, then combine the two and write a blog. Finally, send a recap in the newsletter.

If writing is not your strength, hire someone to put your ideas into words. The most important aspect is that it is getting done consistently. If your grammar isn't perfect, have someone proof it to ensure professionalism of what you send out.

Sometimes, opportunities will present themselves that may surprise you. When I worked at the hospital, part of my role was presenting at the community events. I was interviewed countless times for the local news stations, presented over two dozen lectures, and did interviews for local magazines. All of these activities served one main purpose: to help people find a solution to their nutrition problems. In the end, it increased exposure for me. To this day, I take advantage of any opportunity for an interview or speaking engagement.

Providing valuable content is the gold standard for becoming the expert in your community.

Chapter 9: Establishing Partnerships

Let's imagine you've launched your nutrition business.

You have a steady base of regular clients and a reliable stream of new ones. You could stop there, but should you? When it comes time to expand your program, you need a plan.

It is essential to have a strategy to develop partnerships with like-minded businesses from the very beginning. Take a minute to think about what kind of businesses would benefit from nutrition services. Here are a few examples: corporate wellness, a doctor whose patients need to lose weight, and local restaurants.

At HSN, we have established numerous partnerships over the years. Here is a list of our partners:

- Pediatrician
- Gastroenterologist
- Softball and baseball training facility
- Charter school
- Private school
- Gymnastics training facility
- Adults fitness clothing line
- Kids fitness clothing line
- Four restaurants
- Hair dresser
- A cryotherapy facility
- Chiropractor
- Protein company
- Snack bar company
- Mentoring company

While it will require some extra effort on your part, establishing partnerships will help you expand your reach in your community. Here are a few different kinds of partnerships that have been instrumental in the growth of business locally.

Partnership #1: Physicians and Pediatricians

Doctors know nutrition is important to their client's success. In fact, nutrition plays a vital role in the management of many diseases such as diabetes, Crohn's, celiac, and kidney disease. The issue is doctors do not have the time or resources to provide the support their clients need for dialing in their nutrition. Here is where you can provide nutrition support. (Note: Remember, if you aren't a RD, it is against the law to discuss treating these diseases with nutrition. We tell gyms running our program to refer these clients out if they don't have the dietitian credentials.)

HSN's two largest referral sources come from two partnerships we have established over the years. The first is a pediatric gastroenterologist. I met the doctor while working in the pediatric unit at the hospital. We connected quickly, and he asked if I would see patients at his office. During my lunch break, I would run over and would see a patient. After I finished my shift at the hospital, I ran back over to see a few more.

He encouraged more than half of his patients to book at least one appointment with me. A majority of our long-term nutrition clients have come from his office and have also joined our children's fitness classes after working with me individually on nutrition. He understands the relationship between food and disease management. As parents, we would do anything for our children. If my child was gaining weight and I couldn't help him/her, but his doctor recommended we see a dietitian, that would be the first phone call I made after leaving the office.

Developing a partnership with a physician means a steady stream of clients, and the doctor can be assured that their patient is getting the nutrition support and guidance they need. By staying in communication with one another, you and the doctor can reinforce the message with the client.

For clients that come from referrals, I make calls to that doctor celebrating their success or discussing any challenges I want to reinforce. This way, our plan can be reinforced with the physician.

Partnership #2: Meal Prep and Delivery Services

You will have clients who don't like to cook and eat meals out consistently. If one of their action steps is to meal prep, they are likely to be unsuccessful. Meal prepping is a large time commitment, and some clients will not be ready to take that step yet, so you need a solution for them. Your responsibility is to design a realistic plan to fit into their lifestyle.

Meal delivery companies can provide a short- or long-term solution for your clients who will not spend the time preparing their meals. There is a plethora of these companies out there. Companies will prepare, portion, label, and deliver meals to your client's doorstep.

When partnering with one of these companies, you need the ability to influence the macronutrient and calorie breakdown so clients receive the calories and balance you are recommending. Of course, preparing meals yourself is more accurate, but it's not realistic for everyone to do so.

We've had great success bringing in meal delivery companies for samples during challenges and corporate lunch-n-learns. They provide samples of their products, and HSN receives a percentage of dollars brought in from our clients. It's a win-win for everyone involved.

If you are looking to partner with a meal delivery company, these are questions to ask before you commit:

1. Do they have different portions sizes for the meals including male vs. female?
2. How accommodating are they to different meal preferences? For example, if someone doesn't like fish, are they able to get something else?
3. How often do they cycle their menu?
4. Do your clients have to sign a contract?
5. Are they able to skip a day or two during a week if they go out of town?
6. Do they provide the calorie information for each meal?
7. Are they using synced meal tracking online applications?

Before putting your name behind a company, always try it out yourself first. We have worked with a few different companies in the past and my first step is always to order the food for at least one to two weeks to see if the product tastes good and aligns with what we preach at HSN.

Partnership #3: Corporations

Think about your places of employment, current and past. Would you or your fellow employees benefit from learning more about healthy eating or participating in a nutrition challenge? What would it do to the company morale and relationships with employees?

By working with companies to improve the health and wellness of their employees, you improve the overall well-being of the company, reach a different market besides your circle of current clients, and increase awareness of your entire brand. Employees might attend a nutrition seminar and express interest in personal training or one-on-one nutrition coaching.

It is common for corporations to have wellness budgets as a part of their insurance plan. You can start by offering "lunch-n-learns" where you cater lunch (with the meal delivery service) and provide a nutrition seminar to employees.

Sample Lunch-N-Learn Topics:

- Stress Management
- General Nutrition
- Holiday Survival Plan
- Nutrition for the Whole Family
- New Year, New You
- 10 Steps to a Healthier You

By starting with a lunch-n-learn, you can open the door to larger nutrition partnerships in the future with the same organization. For instance, you can run a corporate challenge; once employees see results, they will continue seeing you for ongoing coaching or might join your fitness facility.

Charging for Corporate Wellness Projects

Corporations will pay for lunch-n-learns, challenges, as well as group fitness classes. Pricing for lunch-n-learns are inclusive with lunch, catered by the meal delivery company we partner with. HSN requires a minimum of 10 attendees to conduct a nutrition presentation on-site, typically charging between $35-45 per person.

Corporate nutrition and fitness challenges are also a way to increase your reach with the nutrition programs you offer. HSN runs six-week challenges at corporations providing nutrition support, meal plans, weekly videos, tracking sheets, and exercise classes. Prior to opening up our fitness facility, we provided classes on-site. Now, corporate employees come to the classes at our facility.

For corporate challenges, start by testing biometrics at the beginning and at the end of the challenge. Provide the company a summary of the improvements achieved by their employees. When the companies see the positive changes, they see the return on the investment and bring you back to do another one.

If a corporation is unable to pay for an entire challenge, provide an option for the employees to pay half, while the corporation pays the other half. The company should provide the prizes for the end of the challenge.

The goal with any corporation is to build relationships that foster long-term clients. Become part of their journey long after a presentation or challenge is complete. If you are a gym owner, you invite the challenge participants to join a free Saturday class or offer the company a team-building event at the gym. You want employees to get their foot in YOUR door.

Partnership #4: Restaurants

Staying on track while eating out is one of the toughest steps for clients when following a new plan. Guide them to safe places to eat out while staying on track with their plan. This can happen through a restaurant partnership.

In your community, there are local, independently owned and operated restaurants around you. HSN and people running our consulting program have had success collaborating with local restaurants to create healthy, "dietitian approved" menu options.

Start with a help-first mentality. You will bring the restaurant more business through your clients and are positioning them as a healthy option for eating out in your community. Approach the owner with your ideas and how it benefits them. This partnership will also provide exposure of your brand to the patrons of that restaurant.

Once the owner agrees, work with the restaurant to highlight healthy options on their menu or make modifications to existing options. The recipes must be compatible with the philosophy of nutrition. Some common changes include adjusting portion sizes or creating a new plate with your company or facility's name. For example, a HSN bowl filled with veggies, grilled chicken, quinoa, and avocado.

The first restaurant HSN partnered with was a seafood place my husband and I frequent. I approached the restaurant as they were redesigning their menu. I worked with them to create and adapt some healthy recipes, and we added our logo next to those dishes on the menu. We held HSN events at the restaurant because I knew people would be able to stay on track. The restaurant also has guaranteed patrons. It's a win-win for both of us.

The restaurant benefits from the clients you send to them and you benefit from exposure of your brand. You might even run a challenge for their employees or invite them over for a class.

Partnership #5: Teen Sports Teams

Nutrition is often the missing piece of the puzzle for teen athletes. Setting up a partnership with a sports team will help to expand your reach and provide athletes with valuable resources to increase their performance.

You can give the team an electronic handbook filled with tips to improve athlete performance that's co-branded with their logo. You can also do a nutrition seminar for athletes and their parents at the beginning of the season.

At HSN, we have partnered with several sports teams over the years. Recently, we established a partnership with an elite gymnastics training facility. We provide an updated handbook every year. We teach nutrition seminars for their athletes broken up by age group every 4-6 weeks. Athletes will try new foods and snacks during the seminars. Parents are sent an email with a video recap of what we discussed and tips on how to implement the information.

The facility pays us for the group sessions and, as well as a retainer for the updated handbook each year. We also work with athletes on an individual basis and parents pay for the additional service. About 20 percent of our nutrition revenue is generated from this partnership and associated referrals.

Finally, we post a highlight photo after the seminar on social media. This helps to increase awareness of the partnerships we have established. You never know who is watching your social media and would be interested in doing something similar for their child's sports team.

Sample Post Recapping Seminar Series:

"Another season has kicked off at Twisters Gymnastics and so has our nutrition seminar series. Best of luck this season, girls! Thanks for having us! #healthystepsnutrition #dietitian #crossfitHSN #twistersgymnastics

Other Partnerships

If you look around your community, there are countless opportunities for collaboration. HSN consulting clients have also partnered with chiropractors, corporations, restaurants, healthy grocery stores, and even local supplement companies. Regardless of who you partner with, do your homework first. You need to ensure your values align with any partnership you develop.

For supplement companies, choose supplements tested by Informed Choice. The FDA does not regulate nutrition supplements, which means the ingredients label might be inaccurate. Informed Choice is a third-party company that tests supplements and matches the actual ingredients to the product's ingredient label.

An Informed Choice-tested product label will look something like this:

However, being tested by Informed Choice doesn't automatically mean it's a great option. Many supplements have a laundry list of chemicals and artificial ingredients listed on their labels. These artificial ingredients will cause bloating, gas, and stomach discomfort.

Evaluate what you recommend to your clients. Our philosophy is whole foods. Steer clients away from replacing meals with supplements. However, there are instances where supplements are needed. Vegetarians have trouble meeting their protein requirements for the day with whole foods alone, so supplementing with a pea protein shake would be an option. Or, a client needs to gain weight. It's much easier to drink calories than eat them, so adding a shake will get them to their calorie goal.

Outside of special situations, I steer clients away from going to supplement stores. Supplement store employees make a commission from what is being sold.

Here is an example of how supplements can go awry: Angie signed up for our OnRamp program. During these four, one-hour personal training sessions, we include nutrition information, as we do for all gym members. We discuss healthy eating, hydration, and what to eat before and after a workout. Angie's schedule is such that she comes to class and then does errands before going directly to work. She doesn't have time to eat after the workout. In this case, I recommended that she have a quick protein shake until her next meal.

Two weeks later, she came in and told me that she was now taking five different types of supplements. Her goal was to lose weight. She was still eating the same amount, but added different types of protein powder after being told by the salesperson at the local supplement store that she needed all these powders. In reality, a simple whey protein was sufficient.

While setting up partnerships is great, do your research and stick with your philosophy; don't rush into a partnership if they do not meet your expectations. Don't lose your integrity over making a quick buck.

Finding Partners

The easiest way to establish a partnership is to get your foot in the door with a mutual connection. Look at your membership base, whether you own a gym or nutrition practice. "Who are your seed clients?" This phrase was coined by Mike Michalowicz in his book, *The Pumpkin Plan: A Simple Strategy to Grow a Remarkable Business in Any Field*. Seed clients are the clients most invested in your product or service and make you the happiest.

Chris Cooper, founder of Two-Brain Business, also describes it as a "help first" philosophy. During one of my first mentoring calls, he asked me to complete the exercise below during one of our first calls; now we have all our consulting clients do the same.

Get a blank sheet of paper and draw a line down the center. On the left side, make a list of the top five clients who are most involved in the services you provide and spend the most money every month using your services. This might be a client who participants in nutrition coaching, challenges, fitness classes, and personal training. On the other side of the paper, write the clients who make you the happiest. It is not surprising that a few names pop up on both sides of the paper. Those are your seed clients.

Take a few minutes to do it here:

Most involved clients/spend the most money:	Clients who make you the happiest:

Start by looking for partnerships with your seed clients. They are bought into your services. They know your philosophy and values.

Here is an example of how one of our seed clients progressed:

Chip called me over four years ago because he was looking for nutrition guidance to change his lifestyle. Chip wanted to lose 40 pounds. He asked if I would come to his house and meet with him and his wife. I didn't do home visits often but decided to in this case. I went to his home and spoke with him and his wife about their eating habits. He started a customized plan.

We discussed all aspects of health and what contributed to his weight gain. His wife is an amazing cook; I know because I have eaten at his house since. We also discussed exercise. I casually mentioned that I'm a personal trainer as well. He came to me for nutrition, but I wanted to plant the seed for personal training as well. Soon after our first meeting, his personal trainer at the time had to stop training him, and so a few weeks later, he reached out to me about personal training three times a week.

Chip progressed in the program and started to see results. After losing 35 pounds, his employees started asking him what he was doing. During our many hours of training, he began picking my brain about how HSN could help his employees. The company decided to run a nutrition challenge; over 30 employees joined the challenge. We tested biometrics at the beginning and at the end, discussed nutrition, distributed meal plans, and led fitness classes on-site two times a week. We also met with the employees every three weeks to discuss nutrition-related topics.

Years later, the agreement with the company has changed, but the results are the same. The employees can attend CrossFit HSN and the company will pay half of the membership dues. If the employee attends more than 10 times a month, they will pay the entire membership. The employees are happy because of the perks, and the company knows the employees will get sick less often and are decreasing their risk of preventable disease. It all started with this seed client.

Starting with seed clients is especially relevant for corporate partnerships. Almost all of HSN's corporate partnerships can be traced back to individual clients that have worked with us either for nutrition counseling, personal training, or CrossFit classes. CrossFit HSN is a small gym with about 80 members in the first year of opening. Of those members, at least 10 percent own their own companies. How could we help their employees and companies through nutrition and fitness programs?

Once someone sees results for themselves and believes in what you do and offer, it's much easier to sell them on getting people in their personal and professional circles involved.

Chapter 10: Common Mistakes

I started working in private practice in 2006 while going to school. In 2012, I opened up Healthy Steps Nutrition. This book is full of the methods I've developed along the way, a system that took years to perfect.

I've made my share of mistakes, and it was those mistakes that taught me the changes I needed to make to be successful. The goal of this book is to teach you how to build a successful nutrition business. You just read the best practices we have developed over the years and implemented at dietitian practices and gyms around the world. Now, let's look at the mistakes I made, so you don't make the same ones.

Mistake #1: Lack of Resources

Earlier in this book, I shared with you what a typical first consult looks like. In that consult, clients are provided with a folder filled with reference materials, including information about the three macronutrients, lists of healthy sources of those macronutrients, customized meal plans, a goal-setting section, and action steps. I didn't always have those folders.

At the beginning of my career, I created resources as I went. I would give clients hand-written notes from our meeting. As you can imagine, references weren't consistent between clients. I didn't have a system in place with a set of resources and tools to provide to clients.

I would review information about nutrition with clients and it would be tough for them to understand how to apply it or remember everything they needed to do when they left my office. This was a mistake because not having tangible resources to give to clients resulted in endless emails and phone calls with questions that could have easily been answered by a simple fact sheet, like "What's a good substitute for broccoli?" The resources I provide now include a space for the client to write down their goals and action steps, another critical component I neglected at the start.

Overall, I was giving clients too much verbal information and goals that were too broad. Instead of saying, "Here are three things to focus on this month," my clients were left with a message that said, "Here are all the things you need to change right now!" Remember, it's a marathon, not a sprint. Just focus on a couple of steps each month. Build a program that's sustainable long-term instead of a quick fix that allows clients to revert to old habits.

Mistake #2: Failure to Set Expectations, Part I

When you're a fresh, brand-new nutrition coach, eager to help people and to build your client base, it's easy to be accommodating to anyone who is interested in your services. When you're concerned about paying the rent each month or when you have a relatively small number of clients, it's easy to fall into the trap of being available to those clients 24 hours a day, seven days a week.

When I first launched my business, I did not set clear expectations regarding the amount of contact I would have with my clients. At all hours of the day, clients would email, call, text or even message me through social media. Imagine getting a text on a Sunday afternoon as you are spending time with your family that you need to call a client right now to answer a question about portion sizes. I've been in this situation more times than I would like to admit.

It's not that I don't want to answer their questions; I do. But, if you don't set some boundaries to guard your time and your personal life, you'll find yourself beginning to resent your clients.

Instead of offering a free-for-all invitation to contact me with any questions, I specify how I can be reached and when to expect a response back. My preferred source of communication is email and I will respond within 24 hours. Mixing client communications across a variety of platforms can also get confusing for tracking client progress.

For your sanity and the overall health of your business, stick to one or two forms of communication and set clear boundaries and expectations from the start.

Mistake #3: Failure to Set Expectations, Part II

Expectations are about more than frequency of communication. You also need to ensure clients understand the long-term goal of your program.

In my case, HSN operates with a two-phase system: initial consultation and ongoing nutrition coaching. In the past, I would meet with a client for their first consultation and often times it would stop after that. They had all the resources to be successful, right? I underestimated the importance of building accountability into our programs. We'd go over the foundations, talk about goals and I'd send them on their way, tossing a haphazard, "Check your calendar; we'll follow up in a couple weeks" as they left my office.

Guess what? People rarely came back.

Today, I'm very explicit about the way our program operates. Phase I, you come in for an assessment and we give you a customized plan. Then, you'll come back in two to four weeks to wrap up Phase I and begin Phase II, ongoing nutrition coaching. We'll schedule a client's next follow-up appointment while they are in my office.

Be clear from the beginning about program expectations. Otherwise, you'll find yourself scrambling for new clients at the beginning of each month. Your clients need accountability and ongoing coaching as part of their plan to be successful. You need ongoing coaching to build a consistent revenue stream from nutrition.

Mistake #4: Underestimating the Value of Content & Social Media

Think about the most restrictive, atrocious FAD you've ever heard of. Despite how unhealthy and horrible it might be, obviously you've heard of it. Chances are it has a following, and social media plays a big role in generating that following.

There's rarely science behind these quick-fix diet solutions, but they're posting success stories and nutrition tips. Suddenly, they're the "experts" and now they have a huge source of income from it. Something is working for them, and it isn't their product.

It works in reverse, too. Consider a great gym. It might have the best coaches and programming in the world, but if a prospective client researches them on social media or a search engine and sees that the most recent post was from a year ago, what is the client going to think? They will assume the gym isn't doing that well or maybe went out of business.

Think about how much research you do on the internet before purchasing an item. Now, take a look at the reviews on your site. Would they prompt you to inquire more or turn you away? When I first started, I underestimated the value of social media. I used it only rarely, and when I did, my posts were not engaging.

As much as you'd like to believe in the philosophy "build it and they will come," you need to promote your business. If you're not posting about your business, people aren't going to find you.

At the beginning, creating content wasn't a priority. I didn't love writing content and would always find something else to do with my time. You need to build your expertise. Providing content to build a following is the best way to help potential new clients. You need to bridge the gap between their problem and your solution.

Mistake #5: Forgetting About Former Clients

What do you do when a client stops coming to you? In the past, I did nothing. Their email addresses sat in some spreadsheet in the archives of my computer, doing nothing except taking up space.

It's an easy mistake to make. These clients sought you out for a reason, and they most likely still need your help. Clients who have seen amazing results and achieved their goals will continue with ongoing coaching. If they don't, they eventually come back for a follow-up. Your past clients need to be reminded that you are there if and when they need your help.

All my previous clients are included in emails and content marketing like newsletters, new programs, special offers, healthy recipes, love letters, nutrition tips, and success stories. If you're constantly in front of people who once had interest in your services, they're likely to come back.

Though it might seem counter-intuitive, your former clients are your best chances at future business. They're the closest nuggets you can grab, because they've already utilized your services. Circumstances will change and eventually they might be ready to start back up again.

Mistake #6: Not Valuing My Time

This mistake is related to Mistake #3.

I used to cater to my clients' schedules, asking them to tell me what day and time works best for them to book a meeting. While this may appear to be good customer service, being too flexible can undervalue your time.

With this method, I would go to the office for a morning consult, have a 10-hour break, then have a consult at night. If you leave your schedule to the whims of your clients, you're sure to be scattered, unproductive, and unsatisfied.

Today, I book clients back-to-back. Clients choose from a few time slots based on my availability so I'm not wasting time. If you're driving 30 minutes to the office for a consult then driving home, that is 1.5 hours of work for only 35 dollars.

Similarly, value your time when it comes to payment. Just because someone makes an appointment doesn't mean they'll keep it, and I've had plenty of no-shows in the past. The client reserved a block of your time. Time that could have gone to another, paying client. You need to protect yourself and the value of your time.

At HSN, we have all clients sign a waiver indicating they understand that we enforce a 24-hour cancellation policy, wherein clients will be charged for any appointment cancelled within 24 hours or for no-shows. In the past, clients have one freebie if there was an emergency, but our clients are very aware of our procedures. This brought our same-day cancellation and no-show rate down to less than five percent. It was 50 percent before the policy was implemented.

I understand that people lead busy lives and sometimes need to reschedule, and for that reason, I send reminder emails the day before a client's appointment. But, if you don't want people to take advantage of you, you need to make it clear that your time is just as valuable as your expertise.

Mistake #7: Not Hiring a Mentor Sooner

As your business grows, investing time and money into figuring out next steps is essential. It is easy to get caught up in the day to day and not consider the long-term vision for your business. After being in business for several years, I finally hired a mentor. I should have done it sooner. In fact, I even wrote this love letter in 2017 about how hiring a mentor impacted our business.

Subject line: We all need a mentor

We are all motivated and excited to get started with something new. But what happens after that excitement goes away? Can you still stay on track?

We ALL need an accountability partner, mentor or someone to keep us from getting distracted from the bright and shiny objects.

Two years ago, I hired a business mentor. It was the best decision I've ever made, besides marrying my husband of course. I'm forever grateful to Sam Brumenschankel for introducing me to Chris Cooper, owner of TwoBrain Business. I was first introduced because he wanted to hear more about our affiliate nutrition program. He was looking for a solution to implementing nutrition programs for the affiliates he worked with and we had been doing it successfully at CrossFit Port Orange.

At the time, I didn't own a gym and had no intentions of starting one in the foreseeable future. I knew I wanted a plan to get out of working at the hospital and run my nutrition practice full time. I was spending so much time driving around between clients and running day-to-day operations of the business that I couldn't even imagine what the realistic next steps would be to get me to my perfect day. He was already helping hundreds of gym owners become successful, but I wasn't sure if he could help me- I didn't own a gym. Boy, was I wrong. I was clearer with my vision of Healthy Steps Nutrition after the first 30 minutes on the phone with him. I decided I needed a mentor and accountability partner. I needed to hire HIM to help me lay out a clear path for my next steps.

Fast forward two years, I left the hospital, opened a gym, wrote a book on running a nutrition business, have a flourishing nutrition practice locally and work with over 125 gyms around the world to implement nutrition. I could not do this alone. I hired a TEAM to help me run the day-to-day operations of both businesses, so that I can focus on what makes me happy.

Before starting with TwoBrain Business, I would have tried to wear all the hats. I could not imagine what my days would look like if we didn't have the eight employees.

Today, I spend the majority of the day mentoring affiliates and helping fellow dietitians grow their nutrition programs. It is the most rewarding job I could have EVER imagined. Through the consulting program I have built at Healthy Steps Nutrition, the reach is so much further.

Yes, it has been a lot of work. Most things that are worth it in the end are a lot of work. Without a mentor, we would not be where we are today.

It's okay to ask for help. It's okay to make mistakes- I've made more than my fair share. A mentor is there to give you a new perspective and help you get to your perfect day.

As you can see, it has not been a smooth journey, and I am grateful for that. The challenges I have had growing HSN have led me to the place where I am now with the company. There is a huge need for nutrition services in every community, and as people make the decision to improve their help, you can be that person or facility. The strategies, structure, and even mistakes outlined in this book will get you to that gold standard nutrition program quicker than you could ever expect.

Guided. Tested. Proven.

This book is just a starting point for anyone looking to implement a nutrition program. There are many essential components to a successful program and HSN has perfected these components to share with business owners around the world. By providing a structured program, resources, and mentoring, HSN's Consulting program does not just set the foundation for a program, but also supports the growth of it.

There is no reason to start your own program from scratch; as a new business owner, you don't have hundreds of hours to create these materials and structures. If you use HSN's turn-key solution, you can spend hours growing your business instead of creating it. If you are looking for more help, you can download free resources and a webinar on the website, https://healthystepsnutrition.com/nourish/.

Andrea Savard, Reebok Combat Training CrossFit

"Kicking off our 2nd 28-Day Nutrition Fix in 3 months. This time with 35 people. $99/pp and this program has netted us close to $8k in 3 months thanks to our partnership with HSN! I'd say that's a nice ROI including full payback of the InBody and the HSN program partnership."

Butch Santucci, Wreck Room CrossFit

"Since kicking off the HSN program a few weeks ago we have added an additional $1800 in revenue. May is looking to be one of our best months yet."

Barry Pepper, CrossFit Port Royal Sound

"In the first 1.5 months of this program, it has brought in over $2500 in revenue. For us the biggest benefit is having the guidance and continued education from someone who has dedicated their life to nutrition and bettering others. For our athletes, it gives them the comfort of knowing that the program they are trusting is not just tested but continually improved upon by an RD."

Jeff Burlingame, Friction CrossFit

"In the first 2 months, the nutrition program has brought in over $2700, 405% ROI. It created a full-time position for a coach!"

Heather Refenes, CrossFit Illumine

"It's really a no brainer. I used to own my own gym and we didn't have the money for programs like this. Or that's what I thought. Now that I am part of HSN, I see that creating your own program is really a waste of time. Time is money for gym owners. Everything Nicole provides is pre-made and ready to launch. Additionally, you can use it exactly as she has it, which is great. Or personalize it, brand it, use it however you want as a gym if you want to spend extra time on it or make it feel more like your own. Nicole is also very accessible and willing to provide additional resources as they are needed. It's a waste of time and effort to do this on your own, and nutrition information and guidance is invaluable to your members."

Appendix A:

Initial Consult Form

Name: ____

Baseline:

C:

L:

E:

A:

N:

Background:

Medical History:

Medications:

Weight history:

Typical Day:

Biometric Testing: Use Biometric Tracking Sheet
Weight, Body Fat, BMI & Measurements

Client Meal Plan Given: _______

	Calories
	Grams Protein
	Grams Carbohydrates
	Grams Fat

Goals:

Action Steps:

Appendix B: Sample Biometric Tracking Sheet

Name: ______________________________

Age: __________ **Height:** __________

Date:				
Weight:				
BMI:				
Body Fat %:				
Blood Pressure:				
Total Cholesterol:				
HDL:				
TC:HDL Ratio:				
Blood Glucose:				
Shoulders:				
Chest:				
Arm:				
Waist:				
Hips:				
Thigh:				
Calf:				

References

1. The Centers for Disease Control and Prevention (https://www.cdc.gov/) is an operating component of the Department of Health and Human Services. Cited statistics regarding adult and childhood obesity can be found at https://www.cdc.gov/obesity/data/adult.html.

2. The World Health Organization (http://www.who.int/en/) is a specialized agency of the United Nations that is concerned with international public health. WHO data on obesity worldwide can be found at http://www.who.int/features/factfiles/obesity/en/.

3. Shai, I., & Stampfer, M. J. (2008). Weight-loss diets—can you keep it off?1. The American Journal of Clinical Nutrition, 88(5), 1185-1186. Retrieved from http://ajcn.nutrition.org/content/88/5/1185.full.pdf html

4. Anastasiou, C. A., Karfopoulou, E., & Yannakoulia, M. (2015). Weight regaining: From statistics and behaviors to physiology and metabolism. Metabolism—Clinical and Experimental,64(11), 1395-1407. Retrieved from http://www.metabolismjournal.com/article/S0026-0495(15)00225-5/fulltext

5. Phelan, S., Hill, J. O., Lang, W., Dibello, J. R., & Wing, R. R. (2003). Recovery from relapse among successful weight maintainers. The American Journal of Clinical Nutrition, 78(6), 1079-1084. Retrieved from http://ajcn.nutrition.org/content/78/6/1079.long

6. The Centers for Disease Control and Prevention (https://www.cdc.gov/) is an operating component of the Department of Health and Human Services. Cited statistics regarding association between cancer diagnoses and overweight and obesity prevalence can be found at

https://www.cdc.gov/mmwr/volumes/66/wr/mm6639e1.htm.

7. The World Health Organization (http://www.who.int/en/) is a specialized agency of the United Nations that is concerned with international public health. WHO guidelines on recommended daily sugar intake can be found at http://www.who.int/mediacentre/news/releases/2015/sugar-guideline/en/.

8. The Centers for Disease Control and Prevention (https://www.cdc.gov/) is an operating component of the Department of Health and Human Services. Cited statistics regarding adult and childhood obesity can be found at https://www.cdc.gov/obesity/data/childhood.html

9. The World Health Organization (http://www.who.int/en/) is a specialized agency of the United Nations that is concerned with international public health. WHO data on obesity worldwide can be found at http://www.who.int/dietphysicalactivity/childhood/en/.

10. The National Institute for Mental Health is a branch under the National Institute for Health (https://www.nih.gov). The Institute is part of the US Department of Health and Human Services. The NIH is the nation's medical research agency. The statistics on childhood eating disorders can be found at https://www.nimh.nih.gov/health/statistics/prevalence/eating-disorders-among-children.shtml.

11. Furry is a website that tracks app and mobile device usage of consumers in the United States. The statistics referenced in this book can be found out http://flurrymobile.tumblr.com/post/157921590345/us-consumers-time-spent-on-mobile-crosses-5.

Made in the USA
Lexington, KY
16 February 2018